# The King of Games

# The
# King of Games

by

## Frank Woolley

*With a foreword by*

## W. H. Patterson

## STANLEY PAUL & CO., LTD.
### Paternoster House - London - E.C.4

MADE AND PRINTED IN GREAT BRITAIN
AT GAINSBOROUGH PRESS, ST. ALBANS
BY FISHER, KNIGHT AND CO., LTD.

# FOREWORD

## By W. H. PATTERSON

### (*Harrow, Oxford University and Kent*)

FRANK WOOLLEY !

I plead guilty at the outset of being very Kent when I say that on no first-class cricket ground in England for very many years now has the speaking aloud of the name of the greatest left-hand batsman England—and Kent—ever claimed been followed by other than an immediate sitting up and taking notice by every lover of cricket.

Men who so far have been talking business, or racing, or what you will, forsake their subject instantly when Frank goes in to bat.

Can there be a surer sign of popularity ?

I am glad to say I have seen all the outstanding cricket personalities of the past fifty years and have played with or against not a few of them. I think I may state that, except the greatest Roman of them all, Dr. W. G. Grace, and K. S. Ranjitsinhji and G. L. Jessop, no cricketer going in to bat has caused such a stir, such a shuffling in their seats on the part of the public, as has Frank Woolley.

It is said that the only person ever heard to express the wish that Woolley would get out—the bowlers always excepted—was a bar-tender.

"While 'e's in," said this temporary out-of-work, arms akimbo, "nobody buys no beer !"

He forgot that the fact Woolley was playing drew many more to the ground than would otherwise be there, so trade gained in the end.

I think it is an accepted fact that the most attractive

batsman in the game for very many years is Frank Woolley. Proof of his attractiveness is to be found in the fact that his brilliant career is not full of individual records, in spite of his numerous great innings.

One record he has and has held for a dozen years, which is to take one hundred wickets and make over two thousand runs in the same season, *four* times. This he did in 1914, 1921, 1922, and 1923. On a point of figures his ten wickets for only forty-nine, five in each innings, for England *v.* Australia at Kennington Oval in 1912 stands out head and shoulders above any other bowling feat in Test history.

As a fieldsman his bag of 994 catches is quite unique.

The most remarkable thing in the career of such a run-getter is that he has only made one hundred for the Players against the Gentlemen. There is still time, happily, to do so at Lord's. From 1913 to 1930 he was never missing from the Players XI there, and captained it twice.

Frank Woolley's batting style speaks for itself—it has done so for years in the unmistakable voice of bat cracking against ball, which is such sweet music to the ears of all lovers of cricket. Woolley's batting at its best has been the Champagne of Cricket, a descriptive term sometimes misapplied to what is really only small beer by comparison with Frank's off-drive or cut. These two strokes of his alone place him high up in the most attractive class, with honours, in the very front seats of the mighty batsmen who have made Cricket. His period in the first-class game, most assuredly the last fifteen to twenty years of it, since he is nothing like on the shelf yet ! will be known as the Woolley era, during which, as regards graceful effectiveness and facile execution, he has stood out supreme.

I must quote here what the late Alfred Lyttleton wrote about the great Racquets player, William Gray. Substituting Woolley for Gray, the words of Mr. Lyttleton apply equally. He wrote :—

"When the greatest masters of various games are passed in review, none seems to have quite equalled Gray in the combination of absolute success with absolute gracefulness. . . . But if perfection in a game be attained by combining success in results with beauty of style—with the exception perhaps of Roberts, the great master of modern billiards whose form, independently of its astonishing results is that of an artist—no one to my mind has brought any game to such perfection as that to which William Gray raised the game of racquets."

To say that with us in Kent Frank Woolley is popular is altogether too commonplace. In Kent Frank is loved, our cricket revolves round him, and has done so for many years. But, in spite of the never-concealed admiration of our sporting crowds, Frank is utterly unspoiled. He is still the modest, unassuming boy of whom that sound judge of cricketers, the late Captain McCanlis, never had a moment's doubt.

For young professionals Frank's life has been a permanent model, loyal to his employers and his captains, quiet, almost shy by nature—a gentleman always.

W. H. P.

# PREFACE

I CAME across recently an old saying that every man has a book in him.

It is not without some diffidence that I attempt to put that old saw to the test. The reader who stays the course to the last page of what is virtually my Life's story will be able to decide for himself which he prefers, Woolley at the wicket or Woolley at the desk. I know which one my money would be on !

I have no sensational tale to tell. In these pages the inquisitive will find no scandal, and no back-bitings. For this I am quietly confident that the best friends of the King of Games will be grateful.

Since Cricket is, at its core, a brotherly game, it has never been false to its proud and unique traditions so long as it has been left undisturbed by ignorant clamour and provocative personal paragraphs.

Mine has been a very happy cricketing life. I do not regret a single hour of it. And I will try to repay some of my debt to Cricket by not now knowingly writing one querulous line.

If I succeed, even only in small measure, in expressing within these pages some of the real Spirit of Cricket, I shall feel I have not written in vain. Because, to myself, as I doubt not to every Kentish man, and to many others, the Cricket of To-day sometimes seems to lack a vital something which was coursing through its veins in its heyday. It appears to me to have lost some of that valuable characteristic which inspired the lines which spoke of the time :

> When crowds will gaze on the game and the green,
> Soberly watching the beautiful game,
> Orderly, decent, calm and serene.

Do, please, let's at least try to get back to that delightful atmosphere. Savouring as it does of church-warden pipes, of long benches, of mugs not too empty, yet not too full, and of friendly chaff and banter—and let personal chit-chat, animosities, and suspicion of knavish tricks go where they will—or our beloved game's ages-long grip upon the English-speaking race will continue to relax. Even, perhaps, unto the final extinction of Big Cricket as a very good reason for public assembly and a recreation in the open air for thousands who love an orderly, decent, calm and serene sport.

The attractive glamour of Test matches apart, Cricket has been loitering for some seasons on the downward path. Or is there no significance in the empty seats which I have seen for some years now at inter-county games which formerly drew large crowds?

Big Cricket, by which I mean Public gate-paying Cricket, has to contend with counter-attractions enough without having to carry the extra heavy weight in its already severe handicap which attaches to inside controversy.

Each successive "incident" adds to the enemies of Cricket.

For that reason alone I take the liberty, in my capacity as senior International professional, to make my appeal to everybody connected with the first-class game, and particularly all who write about it, to do everything in their power to bring about a speedy return to that atmosphere of calmness and jolly good fellowship which was the very essence of Cricket as it was handed down to us.

There have been cases where cricketers themselves have lost interest in the game because of fault-finding and unkindly criticism. Some amateurs have been driven out of the game for practically no other reason. We professionals know well enough that our English cricket is never so strong as when it has a good leaven of amateurs.   It could do with a lot more amateurs than are able, or care, to play to-day.   I am not forgetting that the Saturday start has, I think, played its part in the diminution in the number of amateurs.

Cricket is a well born and bred game.   Therefore, it shuns rather than courts popularity.   For it the gentle and pleasing amenities of the village green, not the braying noisiness of jazz bands.

Let it return with all possible speed to the place it held so proudly in the esteem of all who matter.   I hope I shall see signs of this happening before I have to endure an English summer without the blue sky above my head and the comfortable tread of good Kentish turf under my boots.

I cannot now imagine what an English summer can be like without playing for Kent !

It is, therefore, with no joy that I contemplate the dawn of the day when I start playing the role of permanent looker-on.

I feel now, however, if when that time comes I see half-volleys gently patted back to the bowler that I shall never go to a match again.

F. E. W.

Hildenborough
   Kent.

# CONTENTS

# LIST OF ILLUSTRATIONS

# THE KING OF GAMES

# THE KING OF GAMES

## CHAPTER I

### ONE CRICKETER TO ANOTHER

AN asphalt back yard behind a motor engineer's shop is probably responsible for this book.

Nearly forty years ago four sons were accustomed to emerge from the shop of their father at round about four in the morning, stick a board up against a wall, and take the bat in turns. The godfathers and parents of these four early risers had arranged things fairly by calling two of the brothers Charles and Claude, the other two Frederick and Frank. So there was no work for a selection committee. It was obvious from the start that the C's must play the F's, and play them they did.

One such play I shall never forget. The C's won the toss and made three hundred and eighty, so that, at ten years of age, I tasted the joys of fielding out for a long score. Then our turn came, I was sent in to bat first. Claude promptly bowled me first ball, but my disappointment so overcame him that, saying it was a no-ball, he told me to go on batting. I feel sure he would never have got into an Australian eleven !

I thanked him and remained at the board a week, knocking off the runs myself. For which, in a moment of forgetfulness, Claude punched me on the nose !

Who can say how much the fact of my having defied the opposition for so long at that early age helped me subconsciously in after years for Kent and England ? After all, it is only a matter of degree. A hit for a single or for a four counts the same anywhere, whether in a back yard or on the Angel ground, or at Lord's.

I don't think my big innings was the cause, but all the same it was not long before we had to find another wicket. Broken windows tell such a tale. So we had to move our scanty impedimenta, and in future a gatepost in the lane to the racecourse, which existed in those days at Tonbridge, had to serve as our wicket. Our energy and keenness were not long in attracting other boys, chiefly as rivals of the Woolley quartet. Soon the chaps of about our own age in the village of Leigh, five miles from Tonbridge, became our hottest opponents, and we were not long in becoming engaged with them in a sort of fight for the Ashes !

The Leigh green had a wood on one side of it. We had to get together a team of sorts and walk over to Leigh, carrying our gear. It was on one occasion a baking hot July day when we won the toss. Claude took a stodgy sort of player in with him, and I remember they had made one hundred and ten for the first wicket when Claude hit the ball into the wood. There ended that Test. We couldn't find it—and had to walk home again. Ten miles for me without an innings or a bowl.

It was not very long after that match that I received what I shall always regard as my baptism at county cricket. Between the Angel ground, Tonbridge, and Botney Fields runs a stream. On those fields Tonbridge National School used to play. Our game with them, which we almost invariably lost, was the chief fixture on our unprinted card. I was in my eleventh year when Claude, having won the toss, took me in with him. He proceeded to make 100 while I made 67, and then spoiled the whole show by striking the ball into the stream.

Our game that day ended there, because the headmaster came along to tell us that was the only ball and we'd have to finish the match another day.

On the bank of that stream the curious will find a tree, on four branches of which we brothers each carved our initials. It was from its branches that we used to watch matches.

One day George Cox, of Sussex, was bowling to Mr. W. M. Bradley, with whom really fast bowling was a stronger suit than batting, although he once "cut" Tom Richardson into the pavilion at the Oval! On the occasion of which I write he happened to get hold of Cox's in-swinger and the ball came soaring right over our tree. I thought it a dickens of a hit, while I watched the ball all the way as it went over my head. Quite naturally, I let go of my branch in order to clap—and in doing so went base over end backwards into the stream! Surely a cricketer's baptism.

I got through the next two years somehow, and my first chance came when, at the age of twelve, I happened to be behind the net in which Blythe was practising. On his asking me if I liked cricket, I said, "Yes," and with businesslike acumen, added the information, "I'm a left-hander." That did it. "Charlie" seemed to cotton to me at once, gave me the bat and bowled to me, and then let me bowl to him to the extent of putting sixpence on the wicket and seldom failing to let me hit it at least once.

I owe a deep debt of gratitude to Charlie and shall never forget it. He gave me my first helping hand on the county ground at Tonbridge, and that counts.

Not very long after that first meeting, Tonbridge were one short, when about to play Roughway on the Angel ground. The Roughway captain commandeered me, and I well remember fielding with one eye on the gate hoping the eleventh man would fail to appear. I had to go in last when Roughway wanted twenty to win. We won! I made eighteen not out, and the captain of the winning side, Mr. Tylden, gave me half-a-crown. That was a red letter day, indeed. I was not then on the ground staff at Tonbridge. That

I joined when Mr. Tom Pawley was secretary-manager of Kent County C.C. and Mr. Mason was captain. But my first county match was not until 1906, and well indeed do I recall it.

I missed a brace of catches, quite thoroughly, failed even to catch a skied "no ball," and began right at the bottom of the batsman's class by being out, b Cuttell 0. So I began my first-class county cricket career by being bowled for a blob by a Yorkshireman, though I was playing against Lancashire. These qualification laws !

In addition, my one wicket in the course of 26 overs cost 103 runs, so I could not complain that Mr. C. H. B. Marsham had not given me a good trial with the ball.

I hope I shall escape a charge of vanity if I add that in my second innings I was lbw. b Cuttell 64. This happened at Manchester, and in that game Johnny Tyldesley showed me what batsmanship looks like by making 297 not out.

That game is always remembered by us of the Kent eleven for the amusing end to the Lancashire innings. When Tyldesley had made 297 their ninth wicket fell. He happened to say he'd never made a 300, so, as Worsley the wicket-keeper was coming in our captain asked : "Who can I put on who's sure not to get him out ?" Fred Huish answered at once : "Punter Humphreys, sir." Humphreys was given the ball. He certainly did his best, for he sent down four of the widest balls that were not wides that I have seen. But alas ! the fifth. It went with his arm, and Worsley, going across outside his off stump in imitation of a batsman, saw his leg-stump removed. "Punter" had been on before, during Johnny's flogging, and his analysis read 13 overs, 1 maiden, 111 runs, 1 wicket.

Since then I think I may claim to have had my share of all kinds of cricket, under all kinds of conditions, against almost every race under the sun that takes an interest in the game. Thus, apart from having been bowled, caught, or run out by Englishmen, Scots, Irish and Welshmen, I have been caught by a Frenchman, a Dutchman, a Hindu, a Parsi, a South African, a Singalee, and a Portuguese. I have been run out by a Sikh and bowled by Moslem, Parsi, and Negro. How interesting it would have been had these all been in one team! Together they make up exactly an eleven.

I have played in 922 matches, and made every score from 1 to 111, made 86 "ducks," and two pairs of spectacles, bowled by Tarrant in both innings at Lord's in 1907, and b Brearley and c Worsley b Brearley at Tonbridge in 1909.

In 26 seasons I have "retired" once, and "retired hurt" 3 times.

My aggregate is 54,236, I have taken 2,017 wickets, and have made 994 catches.

I played in 64 Tests in all, 52 of them consecutive against Australia and South Africa.

My highest aggregate is 3,352, made in 1928, with an average of 61.03. My five best aggregates are:

3,352 in 1928
2,804 in 1929
2,643 in 1934
2,344 in 1924
2,339 in 1935

I have been out 36 times in the nineties, with 6 of these at 99.

I have made 141 centuries, 115 of these for Kent.

I have played in first-class matches on 68 different grounds.

My highest score is 305 not out for M.C.C. *v.* Tasmania at Hobart, January 26th to 29th, 1912, when my place in the batting order was number nine—but I went in number four!

I have made eight scores between 200 and 300, the last of them in July, 1935, at the Oval—229.

For Kent I have made 39,658 runs, average 42.55, and have taken 1,526 wickets, and held 863 catches.

I conclude this all too personal narrative with a few words of counsel to young and aspiring cricketers.

It is in all sincerity and with the deep conviction that what I am writing is the cricket truth that I write them.

I beg of young cricketers to lend me their ear, because I feel that of late years not enough of them have taken the game as seriously as they should.

Cricket, I can assure them, is not a game to be fooled at. You cannot play it too seriously, or too directly right up to the hilt of its laws and practices. No matter how light-heartedly you play what is, after all, a game and a recreation, you must, *to make it enjoyable for others and for your side,* both of which must be your first consideration at all times, play it in conformity with its unwritten as well as its written laws.

Its unwritten laws are perhaps more important than some of its written ones. One such is :—

"There is only one captain—obey him, and trust him implicitly, on and off the field—he will not let you down."

You all know that other equally important one :—

"Never dispute, by word or gesture, the umpire's decision on any point."

Remember, if he gives you "out" wrongly to-day, he may give you "not out" wrongly to-morrow. Cricket luck almost invariably balances itself down the years. For example, England and Australia have either each won the toss an equal number of times or are within once or twice of having done so over the whole series.

Refer back to the events of my first county match and do not be too discouraged at a bad start. Lord's was not built in a day. And is not yet complete.

I began with a duck's egg, three dropped catches, and an analysis of one wicket for 103 before I made my first run in first-class cricket.

You young readers are welcome to remember this, because what happened to me subsequently should be an incentive to any youngster and make him realize to the full that there must always be a beginning.

I would also very strongly advise every youngster who happens to do well in his first match, or matches, to be extra chary of taking to heart the flattering accounts he is sure to read about his performance. That is the rough and broken road which leads to the populous town of Swelled Head, believe me. Many have crashed on it.

After a good score or a fine bowling analysis in your first match it is better to go and have a quiet talk with your best friend, your Conscience. He will tell you the Truth without beating about the bush. He will tell you pat that you need not imagine that you will always have such luck ; that the road to sustained success and honours in Big Cricket is a darned hard one ; that it is ridiculous to suppose that you, a half-baked kid, have only to walk out on to "the middle" of a county ground and hit county and perhaps International bowlers about to the tune of, say, seventy runs or even a century, *and for that to be the true form as between you and them.*

I have always a measure of sympathy for any youngster who does something quite exceptional in his first innings. For I know that I found it easier to live up to my first b Cuttell 0 than any colt can ever hope to continue living up to, perhaps, a hundred at the first time of asking.

This applies more to a young batsman than to a young bowler who does something big in his first match. The reason for the difference is this. The young bowler may be a genius. He may be a born Blythe or Rhodes or Grimmett, with some precious property of flight in his bowling which old age alone can remove. Since it is the bowler and not the bats-man who calls the tune in our merry game of cricket, the gifted, or born, bowler has always a greater chance of sustained success than has that very rare individual the born batsman, like Trumper, Macartney, Hobbs or Bradman. These, after all, cannot call the tune, because it is not they who start the game by setting the ball in motion.

Therefore, I warn every batsman who has "come off" at the first time of asking, or who has had a remarkably good first season, to turn a deaf ear to flatterers. Even fond fathers and uncles can do harm here. Remember that the totalling of one thousand runs in a first season is such a rare thing as to justify us in looking on its achievement in the light of a suspicious circumstance. I happened to make over one thousand runs in my second season for Kent, but I did not do so in either my fourth or fifth, and as late as my tenth, failed again to do so. Some of our greatest England batsmen did not record their first one thousand runs until their fourth season, or even later.

I know there is sound cricket sense in the saying that it takes at least three seasons' regular participation in first-class county cricket before a cricketer begins to approach the first-class as a batsman.

I know that I never felt I knew much about the game really until I was about thirty ; that is to say, after I had been playing for nearly ten years regularly. Actually, one is always learning something at it. Yet to-day we read about boys in their early twenties as being the "finished" article ! Except in the case of rare geniuses, nothing could be further from cricket truth. I advise every young man who is contemplating taking up cricket as a profession to ignore absolutely any such harmful suggestion as he may hear or read after he has played a good innings, that he can regard himself as the finished article.

One more topic which concerns the budding professional cricketer. I am and have always been a non-smoker, but I have never been a teetotaller. I would no sooner tell a youngster he must never smoke than I would tell him he must never drink, even though I consider smoking more harmful to the wind and the heart of an athlete than I think alcohol in moderation can ever be. But I do most seriously counsel the strictest moderation in both drinking and smoking, with their almost inevitable accompaniment of late hours. Our forefathers' "Early to bed and early to rise," when acted on, did not help doctors to make fortunes. Strictly followed, it will not keep them now in Rolls-Royces. Eat heartily at the right time of whatever you like best, avoiding only pastries, sweets, ices and sticky things of any kind. Beef is bad to beat, especially if backed up with good English cheese and bread of farmhouse type.

As a final hint, try to "be British" through and through. You can't do better than try and stick to that prescription. It's a winner every time in the end.

I would like any youngsters who really are "listening-in" to me while reading this, to saturate themselves with the favourite verse of the old Cotswold shepherd, Walton Handy, who was on the wireless on Christmas Day, 1934. Here it is :—

> Keep on steadily moving, lads,
> For laziness never will win ;
> May your hand and your heart
> Both play a good part,
> And your motto be—
> *Never* give in.

After writing which, my thoughts fly naturally to memories of my old and dear friend, the late Captain McCanlis.

I believe that I voice every Kentish cricketer who knew him when I say of him that there has been something missing from the cricket of Kent since he died at the ripe age of eighty-five in 1925.

I know that we professionals who grew from boyhood into manhood under his eye and almost in his care, loved the "dear Old Man," as he was always called by us.

Speaking for myself, I say from my heart :

"Thank you, Captain, for all that you did for me by your kindness, your teaching, and your example, in laying the foundation of my very happy career as a professional cricketer."

My introduction to the Old Man happened like this. The details of the incidents of that Monday morning of more than thirty years ago are as clear as though they occurred but last week. Mr. Tom Pawley—I can hear his quick voice now—just said :

"Here, McCanlis, I've got a second "Charlie" Blythe for you !"

"Ha !" replied the Captain, pulling at his beard, rather, as I have heard it said, after the manner of Dr. Grace, who never had a more ardent admirer than our Old Man, "*can* that be so ?"

Then, looking me up and down as he gave me his hand, he added : "Good morning, my boy. Are you a left-handed bowler ?"

On my affirmative reply, he said :

"Then off with your coat, and go and bowl in that second net there."

He stood behind the net silently, and after the quarter of an hour's limit, beyond which he never let a youngster bowl, he called out :

"Now then, my boy, get some pads, put 'em on, and go into number one net."

The reader can imagine my feelings of surprise and pleasure, with not a little fear, when I found the two greatest Kentish bowlers of my time, Charlie Blythe and Fielder, waiting to bowl to me. Well do I remember the first ball. Blythe bowled it, and if ever a ball was bowled on purpose I know in my blood that that one was. It was a peach of a half-volley on the off side.  Bowled specially so that I should get "off the mark."  This is what is meant by the brotherhood of cricket.

I hit it *such* a crack !

I don't know that I liked Fielder's pace quite so much, but evidently I did not flinch, as it was not until this trial had lasted a good ten minutes that Captain McCanlis made a remark.  Then I had given him good reason.  For I had tried the left-handers' natural stroke, and hitting across the flight, missed, and was clean bowled.  Quite quietly, but almost, it seemed to me, before my wicket was broken came the verdict :

"Ha ! my boy, you must cut *that* one right out, and play that ball this way."

There followed a clear exposition of the correct stroke, made with an umbrella.  A few minutes later :

"Now that will do ;  come on."

He met me at the end of the net, put his arm round my shoulder as we walked away, and said :

"You played quite well, my boy.  You would like to play one day for Kent, wouldn't you ?"

To which I replied :

"I would, sir, very much indeed."

And well I recall his reply.  I commend it to every youngster who is on the threshold of a cricket career, as well as to many already embarked on it :

"You will, my boy, you will, providing you always remember," he said in his slow, thoughtful way, *"that you have never stopped learning about cricket."*

I recall trying to thank him, and then he sent me off to do some fielding, and that was the end of my introduction to this remarkable Old Man.

He was a grand judge of cricket, and such a sympathetic friend.  I never knew of him grumbling at any player for a bad stroke.  He was always the first to praise for anything one had happened to do well, and when one struck the bad patch that so far has never

B

missed out any cricketer, and never will, he was wont
to sympathise in his kind old way, with the suspicion
of a twinkle in his eye to add to the encouragement :

"Never mind, you'll make some bowlers' arms ache
for this before long."

Later on in my career I recall him saying :

"Well, Frank, now you have done as I have said
you would, and have played for Kent. Now there's
something more I want to see you do, and that is
to go in first for England against Australia—then I shall
be satisfied."

To my very great satisfaction, he had his wish. He
saw me go in first with Jack Hobbs at Lord's in June,
1930, though that was not the first time I had gone
in first in an Australian Test, as I went in with Wally
Hardinge at Leeds in July, 1921, in the match wherein
Lord Tennyson played those plucky innings of 63 and
36 practically one-handed, having damaged his left
hand so badly that it was all in bandages. He did
that, too, with Gregory and Macdonald bowling !

I can see the dear Old Man at the top of the steps
of the pavilion at Lord's as he pushed his way through
the crowd to pat me on the back, and to say :

"Good luck to you to-day, Frank, my boy," while
his other hand was always working away nervously
at his beard. If ever I longed to hit a hundred it was
on that day, but Fate was against me, as I made
only 41. I had so wanted to do the one thing which
would have completed the happiness of the man who
had done so much for me, but it was not to be. Cricket
runs that way.

I had got well over the settling-down business, and
the first and always awkward quarter of an hour or so
was over. I had got a good sight of the ball, and what
is perhaps more to the point considering all that
success that day meant, I felt like runs. Every
batsman knows that feeling. It is not born of conceit,
or cocksureness, and certainly not of contempt for the

opposition. Nobody but a fool is ever contemptuous of each new bowler as he comes on, because every cricketer knows that the worst ball bowled *can* sometimes get the best of batsmen out. But, for no particular reason I was just not destined to achieve the one thing I most wanted to do. I know one thing well. That I have rarely hit a ball more accurately or so hard as the one off which I was out. That fine steady bowler, Fairfax, was on. He made the ball go away a trifle, but had pitched this one a yard or so short. I cut it according to the copybook. But Tim Wall provided the blotting-paper, and mopped it up at backward point as though I had tossed him an apple.

For my 41 I had been at the wicket something under three-quarters of an hour, after I had lost Jack's valuable company, caught at the wicket off the one from Fairfax that goes the other way, for a single. No doubt I should have got more over the ball I was out to, but batsmen cutting hard cannot be expected to gauge things with mechanical accuracy—or slips and gullies would die of inanition !

Of Captain McCanlis I must say this, in conclusion, that he was just as pleased as though I had made a hundred. But that was his generous and grand nature through and through.

When thinking of him, as I often do in the quiet of an evening, when memories crowd thickly one upon the other, I cannot help asking myself whether the faithful cricket public ever pauses—in these hustle-bustle days has it even time to pause ?—to think as it sees some youngster going in to bat for the first time for his county, what that boy has been through to get where he is ; what he is thinking about as he takes guard ; and what success on this the very door-step of a career means to him ?

No doubt those among the onlookers who are endowed with some of the milk of human kindness, who are not cynics by nature, who can, in fact, think for others, do think about all these things, or some of them, and do wish the boy "the very best." But I'm afraid there are sometimes rather too many of the "did you ever see such a rotten stroke ?" kind of spectator, only too apt to crab and to scoff at failure, but at the same time full of noise at success, always ready to "shout with the winner," which of all traits is, to my way of thinking, the worst. These, unfortunately, are the ones who are most heard. The kind, the thoughtful, ones keep their own counsel. They do not condemn the boy for his failure if he happens to fail. They are the very ones who—they and their like—do the boy good and help the general cause of cricket. They allow for the fact that the youngster has got where he is in almost every case by sheer hard work, and in the teeth of much opposition, and in their hearts they are glad to see success, even small success, reward such real endeavour.

Exceptions to this rule of mine, that only by sheer hard work and in the teeth of much opposition can a youngster get his first trial in his County XI there will always be. Two such are "Charlie" Blythe and Jack Hobbs. The facts of Blythe's first inclusion in the Kent XI have perhaps never been told. So far as I can discover they are as follows. A member of the Kent XI was at the nets at the Rectory Field, Blackheath, in 1898, when Blythe asked if he might bowl a ball or two. Captain McCanlis saw him. That was enough. That gentle, easy run-up, that beautiful full swing starting from almost under his right arm-pit, and that flight could not escape such eyes. "Charlie" was taken on at once, played his first match in 1899 at Tonbridge, and with the first ball he sent down in first-class cricket he bowled the late Mr. Frank Mitchell, finishing with about 5 for 20 on a plumb 'un. He was never left out of the Kent XI henceforth.

Jack Hobbs walked into the Surrey XI after going

through the necessary two years' residential qualification period. At the first opportunity, in 1905, the Surrey Club sent him in first, in the first innings Surrey played in that season, with Tom Hayward. That was against a hot Gentlemen of England side captained by Dr. W. G. Grace, and containing such useful cricketers of those days as Messrs. C. L. Townsend, G. W. Beldam, V. F. S. Crawford, E. H. D. Sewell, W. Brearley, and W. W. Odell. Jack made 18 and 88, and was never left out of the Surrey eleven from that match, unless for injury and illness, until he retired from it at the end of 1934.

These two cases make no difference to the rule that every colt you see in his first county game has got where he is only by hard work, by conforming to discipline, and the general unwritten rules of the game off the field, by studying hard at the nets, and by leading a clean and healthy life. If the youngster has the advantage which I enjoyed under the kindly eyes of Captain McCanlis the sooner will he be fit to represent his county if he himself is any good at all.

No coach can make bricks without straw, though I fear that not a few have had to make the attempt.

But though I disappointed my staunch old friend in the 1930 Test at Lord's, I know from what he said to me afterwards that he was well pleased with the two greatest innings I ever played.

These were my 95 and 93 in the 1921 Test, also at Lord's.

In both cases I was sent in first wicket down, and in both cases England had made a bad start. Whenever asked, I always reply that those two were the best performances with the bat that I have been lucky enough to achieve.

I had against me the three most destructive bowlers of that year, J. M. Gregory, E. A. Macdonald and A. A. Mailey. Also a fielding side than which I do not think I have ever seen a better all-round one. H. Carter, a grand wicket-keeper ; T. J. E. Andrews, a really good cover and as a "silly" point the world's best ; C. E. Pellew, as good in the outfield and at third man as was Victor Trumper or is Don Bradman ; J. M. Gregory, a magnificent slip ; Charlie Macartney, a grand mid-off or in fact anywhere, was in that game often in the deep ; Warwick Armstrong, grand captain, good slip and bluff bowler—18 overs in the first innings for 9 runs and 12 in the second for 19 runs, a total of 30 overs for 28 runs, just think of it, in doing his job "resting" his fast pair ; then J. M. Taylor and Warren Bardsley, both very safe fielders ; and H. L. Hendry, a good slip.

It should be remembered England had just lost 5 successive Tests out in Australia up to March that year, followed by a fair and square hammering by 10 wickets in the first Test in May at Nottingham.

These factors, followed by a bad start at Lord's, confronted me as I walked in to join Dipper, with the board showing 20 for 1. Shortly it looked a lot worse with 3 out for 25, and Dipper and "Patsy" Hendren both out. Mr. Douglas, making 34 at his usual stubborn rate, helped to stay the rout, but after 9 wickets were down we had made but 170, that, too, not due to anything dreadful in the wicket.

I have sometimes thought since then that when I was in the nineties, 9 wickets down and Jack Durston in, that I made a mistake in not going for singles when I had hit Mailey hard. Probably I was right not to let them have a go at Jack, but sometimes these tactics do not pan out as intended.

It is probably sounder in the long run *to take the run if it is there* and trust to the fact that "easy" looking wickets are not necessarily the easiest to get.

Be that as it may be, when the over in which I had hit Mailey without running was nearing its end, it was the fifth ball if my memory has not played me a trick,

I walked into and missed a rather short ball and was easily stumped. Mr. Douglas had made 34, nine of the side had totalled 44, and I had missed my 100 by five runs.

Australia headed our 187 by 155. Next time we made an even worse start when Mr. D. J. Knight was out at once for a single. So I had to face the music for the second time with Gregory and Macdonald with their tails erect and waving ominously !

This time Dipper took a lot of uprooting, and though Mr. Douglas failed, the Hon. L. H. Tennyson, who by the way had come into the team on the recommendation of Commander C. B. Fry, who was offered the captaincy but refused, and suggested the Hon. L. H. Tennyson, made a very robust 74 not out. This time I got to 93, when again it was not one of Arthur Mailey's best that got my wicket.

So I had to make the best of double-nineties at a time when only Warren Bardsley had made double-centuries in Test cricket, his 136 and 130 at the Oval remaining unequalled until Sutcliffe made 176 and 127 at Melbourne on the 1924–25 tour.

The only consolation I had with my two nineties was in knowing that, by a strange coincidence, another left-hander, Clem Hill, the great South Australian batsman, had had an even more excruciating experience in 1902 in Australia. In three successive Test innings he made :

        c Jones b Barnes...................... 99
        c Tyldesley b Braund.................. 98
        b Jessop ............................. 97

Ten years later I fielded while Clem Hill made 98 in the third Test of our 1911–12 tour in Australia. So, after all, there is nothing new under the sun, and who am I that I should complain of my bad luck at Lord's in making 95 and 93 !

Before leaving this particular 1921 Test I must refer to a matter about which I have felt inclined once or twice to write to the Press but have refrained.

Those who saw that Test may perhaps remember that I was hit by the ball bowled by Gregory or Macdonald on three or four occasions.   When the Body Line campaign during the M.C.C.'s 1932-3 tour in Australia was at its height I recall reading more than one reference to the tactics of Gregory and Macdonald in that game.  I regretted very much that anyone should have taken it upon himself to complain publicly that these two bowlers had bowled "at" me. I still regret that such complaints were made.

If there had been any necessity to complain, surely I was the only one entitled to make the complaint ?

I did not complain, I have never complained, at what happened.  For the sufficing reason that there was nothing to complain about.

I am entirely unaware that either bowler bowled "at" me.

I am well aware that I was hit—quite painfully aware at the time !—*because of my own mistiming*.

That which made each hit sting more was the fact that in each case I was hit by a ball that ought to have been scored off.

Every cricketer knows that sometimes it is quite unavoidable that he should make choice of the wrong stroke for the particular ball bowled.  In doing so he is likely to get into the wrong position, and in fact often does so, for the ball which he has to deal with. His feet have moved, and he has assumed a more or less "set" position once his mind is made up.  The fact that he has become so "set" does not matter so much if it is a slow or a medium-paced bowler who is bowling.   But when the ball is advancing over a distance of something round about 60 feet at a speed of between 75 and 90 feet per second the prospect of re-moving your feet to take up another position—

which, too, must be the correct one this time—is somewhat remote to say the least of it. Now, Mac-donald was then one of the two fastest bowlers I have ever met. He was in 1921 certainly faster than Lar-wood then was, and probably faster than Larwood ever was. Consequently, any cricketer will be able to visualize what happened when I was struck in the back or high on the hips. He will understand that it was quite possible—and this is, in fact, what actually did happen—for me to mistake the ball which goes with the bowler's arm, on to the body or the leg-side of a left-hander, for that ball which all fast bowlers send down, the ball which goes across to the off-side of a left-hander.

To play this last ball correctly I *must* move my back foot across the wicket in front of the off-stump in order to get over the ball in case it rises sharply from the pitch. Having done this to a fairly good length ball that I had expected to go across just out-side my off-stump what is the next thing to be done if that particular ball, on pitching, instead of going on *as expected* introduces the element of surprise, which is more than half the charm of cricket, and proceeds to go "with the arm" on a line on to or just outside my leg-stump ?

Obviously, unless a left-hander so "caught," either by the bowler's cleverness, or by some inequality where the ball pitched which caused it to perform the unexpected, is extraordinarily agile with his footwork, or lucky in that the ball "went" abnormally towards the on-side, he is "for it."

That, too, because the bowler was clever, not malicious.

I do not for one moment believe that either Gregory or Macdonald bowled "at" me in that match.

That I have in my time been the subject of such attentions on the part of a few bowlers of some speed I am satisfied. It would serve no good purpose were

B*

I to name them. They and I probably finished up fifty-fifty ; perhaps every now and then the scales were a bit down on my side, as I happen to rather like the fastish ball that would crack me in the ribs if my bat was not in use. One cannot take part in nearly a thousand first-class matches without having been stung up now and then.

In my estimation a great deal too much fuss is made when a batsman is hit. After all, few bowlers are fast, and most blows are glancing blows.

It has also to be borne in mind that the majority of players nowadays are protected by thick pads under their clothing as well as over their legs. This weak practice has come into the game since the War. It is greatly overdone, and I feel sure hampers the wearer considerably. For many years at the beginning of my career when there was much more, and in many cases faster, fast bowling than there is now I never wore any kind of protection except pads. After all, the bat is the thing to play the ball with.

I am inclined to think this padding up defeats its intention.

It may be the cause of some of the bad batting one sees.

A padded player, relying on his armour, may get in the habit of not playing *at the ball*—or at all events, playing carelessly because he thinks he is immune from injury. Hence the frequent injuries we read about annually in these days.

This is a matter worthy of the serious notice of coaches, captains, and the players themselves.

Perhaps I have been one of the lucky ones, for I have "retired hurt" only three times, and have retired only once in 922 matches.

It is my considered opinion that in almost every case the fact that the batsman has been hit has been due either to his own mistiming, or to clumsiness with his bat.

The facts of cricket bear me out. It is said that the great Ranjitsinhji *complained of his own bad play whenever a bowler managed to hit him on the pad*.

It is known that in a famous Gentleman *v.* Players match at Lord's, which the amateurs won by the fine fast bowling of Messrs. N. A. Knox and W. Brearley, Tom Hayward made a hundred and was not touched by the ball, while none of the other members of his side could get a score worth mentioning.

More recently during the M.C.C. tour of 1932–33 in Australia, Don Bradman *was only once hit, and that on the forearm, by a ball from Larwood*, who the Australian Press alleged was doing little else but bowl "at" his man, and at Bradman especially.

Another notorious instance was the century made by Mr. D. R. Jardine against the West Indians at Old Trafford in 1932, when Constantine and Martindale were supposed to be bowling "at." Mr. Jardine, unscratched, played the "at" stuff with his bat, proving this can be done.

From time immemorial batsmen have been severely hit by the ball from fast bowlers. These minor hurts will continue for so long as the diminishing race of fast bowlers has a representative in first-class cricket. It would be a bad thing for the game were it otherwise. Cricket would soon lose its attraction if bereft of its only thunder.

It is not less fast bowling that is needed, but a good deal more of it.

When I made my bow in first-class cricket one was sure of having to cope with a really fast bowler in practically every county match, sometimes two of them. But, in those days, captains did not make the mistake of placing all their eggs in one basket by bowling their fast men in pairs, thus tiring both out simultaneously.

No, they always put on a fast bowler at one end, and, if possible, a slow left at the other. Thus compelling the batsmen to play two games, more or all the time.

Of course, there were exceptions to this rule, but I do know that Kent were never so strong as when Blythe and Fielder shared the bowling. We have never been so strong since, for all the grand length and stamina of "Tich" Freeman.

Armstrong's was a special case in 1921. He had just smashed up England on hard wickets in Australia, mainly, it is true, to Arthur Mailey's 36 wickets in the rubber. But the first Test here of 1921 had shown him his path. Gregory and Macdonald took sixteen wickets in that.

Armstrong would have been crazy not to have continued to play his fast bowling card for all it was worth. Especially as wickets continued to be hard.

So, naturally, he began with them at Lord's, where they took thirteen wickets ; continued with them at Leeds, where they took ten ; and then, having won the rubber, saw a mud wicket in the famous two-day Test at Manchester (in which Armstrong made history by bowling two overs in succession from the same end !) handicap his fast pair, who between them then took one for 191 runs. Both were on first again, however, at the Oval, where they took 6 for 304, but as Warwick was reading a newspaper in the deep field on the third day it may be he was unaware who was bowling in our second innings.

That was the Test in which Philip Mead also made history with 182 not out, the highest individual score in Test matches in England, until "the Wrecker" came along in the shape of Don Bradman to gaily gallop a coach and four through one after another of all of our individual Test records, from the late Mr. R. E. Foster's ⁾seemingly invincible 287 at Sydney in December, 1903, downwards.

Though I have seen fast bowlers in pairs successful enough I can never bring myself to believe that such tactics are such good cricket as that seen when a very fast and a very slow bowler are sharing the attack.

Next best is such a pair as were Barnes and Mr. F. R. Foster, who though much of a kind as regards actual pace, were entirely different types to play. Their bowling on the 1911–12 tour in Australia, when Mr. Douglas had to take over the captaincy because of Mr. Warner's illness, was the most destructive in my Test match experience. I have just given the Gregory-Macdonald figures for 1921. In 1911–12 Barnes, who was not put on first in the first Test, and Mr. Foster who was, did the following damage :

| | | |
|---|---|---|
| First Test, | Sydney | 11 wickets for 376 |
| Second Test, | Melbourne | 15 wickets for 283 |
| Third Test, | Adelaide | 14 wickets for 315 |
| Fourth Test, | Melbourne | 14 wickets for 236 |
| Fifth Test, | Sydney | 12 wickets for 260 |

A really grand total of 66 wickets, out of a possible 100, for 22.7 runs each, a really wonderful average over a series of ten innings in Test cricket on the Australian pitches of those days. They are different wickets now, I am told, being not so fast and not quite so faultlessly true.

I am able to write enthusiastically about that fine combined bowling performance because I was one of the favoured ones who was able to watch it from a seat, so to say, in the front row of the stalls. I saw it all from the slips where, in the Fifth Test, I twice caught Trumper off Barnes, and made altogether six catches in the match, two each off both these great bowlers in the second innings.

It was on that tour that I met, in my opinion, the greatest of all the googlie bowlers, Dr. H. V. Hordern. Next to whom I class A. E. Vogler of South Africa and Gordon C. White, also of South Africa, as the most difficult. Hordern bowled his "googlie" faster

than any of the others. I fell to him twice in my three
innings in the first two Tests, but though he did not
get me again in the remaining four innings which I
played in the last three Tests I do not claim to have
"found" him out because of that. Perhaps his early
successes made me more careful, anyway I made 133
not out in the last Test in an innings when he took 5
for 95, following this with 5 for 66 in our second
innings.

But nothing he, Trumper, Bardsley, Armstrong or
Ransford could do could stop our famous bowlers
winning the rubber for us with four wins one defeat.

But for a sad, but understandable, error of judgment on the part of Mr. Douglas, I believe we should
have done that which no English side has yet achieved,
and that is to win all five Tests in Australia.

Owing to the illness of Mr. Warner, Mr. Douglas
was captain from the first Test, which took place at
Sydney. We lost the toss. Perhaps the whole story
of how Barnes was not put on to bowl first with Mr.
Foster has never been told. As I walked out alongside
Barnes as we went out to field I am able to give it
here, and thus to deny at least one of the silly yarns
that was put about, viz., that because Barnes was not
given choice of ends he practically refused to bowl and
had to stand at backward point until he got over his
bad temper. There is no truth at all in that tale.

What actually happened was that Mr. Douglas came
up to Barnes, as we were walking out, and said :

"I'm going on first, Sid, as I think I shall be able
to make it swing a bit."

Barnes seemed naturally a bit taken aback, but he
took his disappointment well, when he replied :

"Oh, that's all right, but what am I out here
for ?"

To which Mr. Douglas said that he'd only have a
few overs, as he might get a quick wicket with the
new ball. It was then that Barnes might have remained

silent, or have worded his remark differently as he said :

"Well, if you're going to bowl with the new one, you can jolly well go on with the old one, too."

However, there was no ill-feeling between these two, and in the end Barnes bowled more than double the number of overs sent down by our skipper, and was always put on first after the first Test. Mr. Douglas was a good enough bowler, however, to get ten wickets with the "old ball" in four Tests after having taken 5 for 112 with the new ball in the first one.

Both the Melbourne Tests of that tour stand out. In the first one, on December 30th to Jan. 3rd, 1912, Barnes made history with the following opening :

| | |
|---|---|
| W. Bardsley b Barnes ................. | 0 |
| C. Kelleway lbw b Barnes ............ | 2 |
| C. Hill b Barnes ...................... | 4 |
| W. W. Armstrong c Smith b Barnes .... | 4 |

Of course, England won that Test, especially as Trumper was b Foster 13 and b Barnes 2.

Then, in the February 9th to 13th Test at Melbourne, the following pleasing picture for English eyes came to be painted by two great artists :

| | |
|---|---|
| J. B. Hobbs c Carter b Hordern ........ | 178 |
| W. Rhodes c Carter b Minnett ....... | 179 |

This famous pair, the best pair of runners between wickets in my experience, created the World's Record Test partnership for the first wicket of 323. It is scarcely credible that Australia only let us total 589 in that innings. Such is their intensive sticking power, while we Englishmen simply do not go on and on scoring as Australians do in similar cases. It is true that the dismissals for a ducks' egg apiece of Jack Hearne and Mr. Douglas made all the difference to us, but George Gunn 75, Mr. Foster 50, and myself at number seven in the order 56, all got well in and should have made a lot more.

However, we won by an innings and 225, so did well enough in the end, due mainly to a 5 for 46 from Mr. Douglas.

Jack Hobbs had 126, 187 and 178 in successive Tests on that tour, finishing an easy first in the averages with 662 total and an average of 82.75 to Rhodes' 463, average 57.87, and my own 289, average 48.16.

Jack was a mighty big proposition in those days, when he was a far greater batsman than the Hobbs who is known only to post-War watchers.

Then he seemed at his best to have two strokes and plenty of time for every ball bowled.

His consistently easy and sure method of playing the googlie was unsurpassed.

I am unaware where in the list Jack places Dr. Hordern among the googlie bowlers, but while the Doctor made no impression on Jack in the first two Tests, when he scored 63, 22, 6 and 126 not out, Jack was out four times in his last five Test innings of that tour to Dr. Hordern. His last five innings were 187, 3, 178, 32 and 45, and Dr. Hordern got his wicket the last four times he batted. Rhodes, on the other hand, after going in first with Jack, which he did not do in the first Test of that tour, in which Dr. Hordern got him in both innings, was never out to the Doctor in the remaining seven innings.

The surprise of that tour was undoubtedly J. W. Hearne, for after beginning his Test career with three scores of 76, 43 and 114, he played six more innings with 18 as his highest score. This artistic off-side player never again touched that early form owing entirely to the effects of ill-health. A fine player of fast bowling and a right-hand bowler who really spun the ball, "Young Jack" would have been a world beater as an all-rounder had he been endowed with the robust health which others have enjoyed. When his history comes to be written, I hope the Essex eleven of his best days, headed by Mr. Perrin, will be persuaded to contribute a chapter. They could probably write a lot about "Young Jack's" bowling, not to mention his batting, even though they seemed to know nothing about the former !

I have rambled on at length here about the 1911–12 tour in Australia because it was, on the whole, the most memorable, perhaps because it was the first, I ever had the pleasure of sharing in. Other Test reminiscences appear in later chapters.

# CHAPTER II

## MEN OF KENT AND KENTISH MEN

Cricketers are all brothers ; such I count ye.
Your Cricketer no cogging practice knows.
No trick to favour friends or cripple foes ;
His motto still is : "May the best man win."
Let Sussex boast her Taylor, Kent her Mynn ;
Your Cricketer right English to the core,
Still loves the man he has licked before.

THE above lines were spoken at the Canterbury Week Festival in 1842 at the first performance of the Old Stagers. In case my quoting of them should alarm any nervous reader that I am about to write my version of the History of Kent cricket, I hasten to calm him by giving my assurance that I have no such intention. I am indeed unfitted for the task, as I have been otherwise rather too busy to absorb enough of the not inconsiderable literature of my county to qualify me for such an undertaking. Reference to the past is, however, necessary here and there. So I have begun with the lines, which in my opinion, breathe the spirit in which we of Kent go to the wicket. Each of us doing his best to carry on the grand tradition which has been handed down to us by our greatest cricketers and captains from our seventeen-stun fast bowler, Alfred Mynn—

Proudly, sadly, we will name him,
  To forget him were a sin ;
Lightly lie the turf upon thee,
  Kind and manly, Alfred Mynn

—down to our much beloved recent friend and President, Lord Harris.

It is in no boasting spirit that I state my belief that we in Kent do play cricket in a spirit rather characteristically our own. To us a defeat is not a case of the skies falling and of the near end of the world, but rather of : "Well done, ——shire, good luck to you, you put us where you wanted us this time, next time we hope to return the compliment."

In Kent we have, thanks to the then Duke of Dorset, who gave them their ground, the oldest cricket club in the world, Sevenoaks Vine. Its opening date I do not know, but there is record that the Vine club was playing in 1734, because, two years ago, its Bi-centenary was celebrated.

Nor is this the earliest instance of cricket being played in Kent, as, in his book published in 1672, a clerical gentleman writes of "cudgel playing, stoolball, crickets, and many other sports" having been played in Maidstone, which he describes as "formerly a very prophane town." I cannot endorse that opinion, although on the old Mote Park sloping wicket I must confess to having heard observations on the part of members of visiting teams who had failed to connect in fourth innings which were a trifle free.

Not only is the Vine the oldest cricket club in the world, but it is probable that the first cricket bats ever sold were sold by a Sevenoaks bat-maker, named Pett, who kept a toyshop. He charged four shillings and sixpence per bat. Though the price makes one's mouth water a lot, I imagine that if used to-day the implement itself would make one's fingers sting a lot more.

We in Kent owe everything to the gentlemen of the County, who in bygone times took into their employ men who could play cricket well.

Interest in the game thus created has never left Kent, and though we have won the Championship only four times—1906, 1909, 1910 and 1913—and in every such success I had the honour of sharing, I am satisfied that the public's interest in the game was never keener than it was last year, 1935. Then only for a short time did our Eleven look like making a real fight for it for first place in the Championship. So that it is but the bare truth I state when I assert that, Championship or no Championship, the Kent County Cricket Club will live on.

Our public is a grand one for applauding the losers as well as for not forgetting the winners. I hope I shall be acquitted of any inclination to write in a parochial spirit when I state that there is not, take it all round, a more sporting, or fairer, or enthusiastic a public, or one so faithfully loyal to the very best interests of cricket as it ought to be played, than is the public which is to be seen, whether the Kent Eleven is near the top of the tree or not, on any of our Kentish grounds. I know they play the game by us, their players, right up to the hilt, applauding us when we come off but never failing to show the sympathy of sportsmen when we don't. Kent has been called the Garden of England. We of Kent's Eleven do our best not to sully that proud title, and I must say our efforts are nobly seconded by the demeanour in general of our cheery public. I know and feel that I personally owe a great deal to the kind support and encouragement they have always given to me.

I am not permitted to mention his name, but an old cricketer, whose judgment would command respect in any company of cricketers, gives me the following best possible Kent XI chosen only from men who have represented Kent in the last fifty years. His batting order would be as follows : Lord Harris (capt.), W. Yardley, K. L. Hutchings, Woolley, W. H. Patterson, J. R. Mason, A. P. F. Chapman, Ames, Freeman, Blythe, Fielder.

I feel that this selection may interest the Old Brigade

as much as the New, for it is a sure thing that in a county like ours many of the public will have their favourites, and they won't hear of these being omitted from such a fancy selection. I cannot, of course, speak from personal experience of our past great, but the team here chosen contains our best batsman-wicket-keeper, Ames ; our best slow left-hander, Blythe ; our best all-round right-hander, Mr. Jack Mason ; and our two greatest fieldsmen, Messrs. K. L. Hutchings and A. P. F. Chapman.

If I had to decide between Mr. W. M. Bradley and Fielder, I would choose the last named because of his batting ability. Not only did Fielder help to win the second Test of the 1907–8 tour in Australia at Melbourne, by one wicket, making 18 while Barnes made 38 not out when all seemed lost, but he helped me to put on the record tenth wicket partnership in England of 235 for Kent v. Worcestershire in 1909 at Stourbridge. This record stands to-day, twenty-seven years later, in England and is only beaten in the world by the 307 of A. F. Kippax and H. T. Hooker, *off eight-ball overs* in 1928–29, for New South Wales v. Victoria.

Fielder made 112 not out in our record stand and my score was 185.

I have good reason for remembering that partnership because after I had made 16 I went down almost on my right knee to pull Arnold to leg, but mishit. The ball went off the shoulder of my bat on to my lip, badly splitting it, and giving me a fat nose into the bargain. I had to leave the field for repairs and we had lost two wickets at the time. After four or five more had fallen, Mr. E. W. Dillon came to me and said : "What about it, Frank ? D'you think you can have another go ?"

"Yes," I said, "I'll have a shot."

In I went again and we had about 70 to save the follow-on, so far as I recall, when Fielder joined me. As the saying is, he didn't half play an innings !

Nothing but the middle of the blade for him that day.
Not only did we save the follow-on, but we won by an
innings after Worcestershire had made 360, Pearson
making a jolly good 160.

And so I go on with my innings, writing at the will
of my memory and of the thoughts which follow one
another as I sit before a fire on bleak January days,
pondering the past and anxious for April to hasten
her leaden feet.   Whether one is a man of Kent or a
Kentish man depends, so I am told, upon whether one
is born north or south of the Medway.

More fortunate am I, without a doubt, than was
that cricketer who first saw the light in a room half
of which is in Kent the other half in Surrey.   A fact
that did not escape Lord Harris when the cricketer in
question started to knock Kentish bowling about at
Blackheath !   After all, what is the use of a frontier if
it doesn't matter which side of it you were born, or
live ?   Kent has never played an unqualified cricketer.

Mention of Surrey reminds me of my first match at
the Oval in 1906.   I went to the famous ground almost
trembling.   I had never even seen Tom Hayward, but
I had heard of the Oval wicket and of his habit of
going in to bat at twelve o'clock and remaining there
pushing the ball about at will until he'd had enough.
My shivering did not lessen noticeably when we lost
the toss.   Fielder and I were put on first.   We were in
luck's way, because after about an hour and a half's
play six wickets were down.   I think I must have been
by then in some kind of an unconscious condition,
because I remember taking advantage while the field
was changing ends to almost whisper to Fielder :
"When's Tom Hayward coming in ?"

"Tom ?" said Fielder.   "Why, you bowled him second
ball !"

Fielder had seven and I three wickets in that innings,
and we got rid of Surrey for 73.   Kent then made 137,
of which my score was 72.   No wonder I like the Oval

wicket. That was my first innings there, and my last, last season, produced 229, after an interval of 29 years.

But my interest in that match did not end there, for I took 6 for 39 in their second innings ; while, in our second, we found ourselves battling to such an extent that when Fielder came in we wanted 19 to win.

That, too, after getting such a side as Surrey out on the Oval for 73 runs.

It was now my job to keep the bowling away from Fielder ! Gradually a run or two came along until there remained 10 to get. But Fielder had the bowling. He had a crack at the ball, and not heeding that it was going dangerously near cover came full pelt up the pitch. So I ran also, cover fielded and flung in wide, and the four overthrow made it a five, with me to face Walter Lees.

He set the first crows-round-a-bone field I had ever seen. There were two of the "silliest" points, short third man, and two short legs as well.

But Fielder did not have another ball to play !

Lees bowled the first three too wide on the off for me to take the risk. Then I decided something had to be done, and at least I must get to the other end. So, at the fifth, another widish one, I had a good welt, to see the ball go over cover, crack, first hop into the crowd. Again, at the sixth, holding the bat high up, I let go as hard as I could. The handle slipped in my hand, but the back of a bat is just as wide as the front, and the ball went off it over slip's head for four and we had won.

In the whole of my career I have never had such a half-hour as that which followed. Before I had moved towards the pavilion Fielder was two-thirds of the way there so I thought it time to hasten. The crowd was swarming on to the ground. Somebody stole my bat (this was returned later), and whether in excitement or not I shall never know, but I got two proper whacks from an umbrella on my shoulders and back of the neck as I entered the pavilion gate and turned to the right towards the dressing room. In those days we did not go up the steps and enter the dressing room by the balcony as to-day. Somebody—I know not who—pressed two sovereigns into my hand, and by the time I was able to reach the dressing room I really hardly knew what I was doing. All sorts of people were shaking me by the hand, and at the finish, probably in my hurry to escape, I actually got into my bath with one boot on! My score in the second innings was 23 not out, so that in my first Surrey match I made 95 for once out and took 9 for 76.

At that time the *Daily Mirror* was giving eight-guinea awards for the best performance of the week, and when that came along to add to the mysterious two pounds already mentioned, plus my match fee and talent money, I decided that I'd had a pretty good match. Yes, I like Kennington Oval.

That was not the best bowling performance I brought off against Surrey at the Oval, where, generally speaking, left-hander bowlers are not noticeably successful. My best analysis against Surrey there was in 1911, and it reads :

6.3 overs, 3 maidens, 9 runs, 7 wickets.

I wrote just now that I hardly knew what I was doing when I got back to the dressing room. That such a thing is quite possible is shown by the astonishing performance on one occasion at Trent Bridge of Ashdown. George Gunn was batting to Ashdown's bowling, and in his well known seemingly careless way George walked in to quite a decent length ball and let fly. He happened to hit it almost straight back at Ashdown's face. The bowler, partly off his balance, seemed to cross his arms in front of his head as a shield rather than to attempt the catch. However that may be, the ball hit the palm of his right hand, and stuck. Ashdown turned round, walked back to the beginning of his "run," and started to run up to bowl the next ball. Gunn was by this time many yards towards the pavilion and one or two of us had sat down.

"Hullo!" said Ashdown. "Where's George?"

The bowler *actually did not know* that he had made a catch!

Another, though a different kind of instance of—shall I call it?—temporary unconsciousness of a player occurred during a match wherein I had one of my earliest experiences of Mr. Walter Brearley, who was often a thorn in the side of Kent. The fun, for us, began when, after we had made a good score at Manchester, Lancashire had nine out for a small score, and it remained for Mr. Brearley and Cook to right the ship. Mr. Brearley hit the first ball toward cover, and off they went, quite regardless. Both, however, were so intent upon the fieldsman that they crashed together at mid-wicket, both going down almost as though in a Rugby tackle.

"Why can't you look where you're running?" cried Mr. Brearley. "Next innings you can bally well bowl 'em out yourself."

How we laughed, as Huish broke the wicket. In Lancashire's second innings they wanted about 200 to win when it became Mr. Brearley's turn to bat. He jumped the pavilion gate as usual and came striding in, the crowd roaring its approval. Blythe pitched one up, Mr. Brearley hit it to me at cover. I threw in hard, the ball bounced through Huish's hands and was fielded by Jim Seymour, after running across from slip. He flung to the bowler's end towards which Mr. Brearley was now making haste. The ball hit him plumb on the back of the head and, going down like a log, he lay motionless. There was a dead silence, during which Mr. Dillon rushed up and said:

"Come on, get up, Walter," to Mr. Brearley, who had begun to move.

Pushing Mr. Dillon aside, he bounced up with a :
"Who's the b— fool who threw that ball ?" rubbing
his pate as he glared around.   Poor Jim, he had to
come forward and express his regret at the bad shot
which had caused so much amusement, to all but Mr
Brearley.

### MY TWO PAIRS OF SPECTACLES

It was this Lancashire bowler who presented me
with one of my only two pairs of spectacles.   This
occurred at Tonbridge in 1909, when I had one of those
really bad matches which come to us all in turn.   My
share in it is set down here as an example to young
players what they may expect to happen to them at
any moment.

| | O | M | R | W |
|---|---|---|---|---|
| Woolley b Brearley ..................... 0 | | | | |
| Woolley c Worsley b Brearley ........... 0 | | | | |
| First innings .............. | 9 | 0 | 27 | 0 |
| Second innings .......... | 9 | 0 | 31 | 0 |

There's a nice egg collection for you !   I could not
even produce a maiden over !   I was in perfect health
at the time, as was apparent when in my next innings,
against two such really fine very fast bowlers as
Burrows and the late Mr. W. B. Burns, I made 60
against Worcestershire, also at Tonbridge.

The bagging of a "brace" is not a difficult matter.
After the second duck the disconsolate batsman, as
he wends his way to the pavilion gate imagining a pair
of eyes in every blade of grass, should remember the
plaintive epitaph—

> Since so quickly I was done for,
> I wonder what I was begun for ?

and not forget that there is always a to-morrow.

The following month I made 185 against Worcester-shire at Stourbridge, that time when Fielder and I put on 234 for the last wicket and 117 against Surrey at Blackheath. Thus the spectacles were very soon lost in oblivion.

About my first "pair" there was a remarkable coincidence. It happened at Lord's in May, 1907, in a match, Kent v. M.C.C. Tarrant, the Australian left-hander, bowled me in both innings. In both innings I had five overs from Tarrant, not another ball from any other bowler, and was out in both innings to the last ball of the fifth over.

That is one side of the picture as it concerns myself at Lord's. On the brighter side I have that brace of nineties in the 1921 Australian Test, and there is also an effort with the ball, for Kent, which I always think of when the well-worn theme of a match not being lost until the last ball has been bowled crops up. This occurred in 1908, the year after my Tarrant "brace." Mr. Jack Mason was captain. Both sides had made decent scores, and it was after a quarter to six on the third day, when, Middlesex having lost only four wickets, the game was as good as drawn. Our skipper came up to me and said : "Tired, Frank ? If not, go on at the top end." I did so. Result :

| O | M | R | W |
|---|---|---|---|
| 4.3 | 2 | 8 | 6 |

It takes me less, on average, than two minutes to bowl an over, so that in roughly eight minutes' actual bowling I had finished the match, though, allowing for five batsmen to come in, the time taken must have been about twenty minutes.

Mention of the time taken over bowling an over calls to mind the almost daily inaccuracy in accounts of matches when the length of spells of bowling or batting is recorded. If a bowler is put on at twelve and taken off at one o'clock it is always said he has bowled "for an hour." Actually, he has bowled for half an hour ; still less if wickets have fallen or the bowler at the other end takes longer over an over than he does. Similarly, a batsman's innings is spoken of as, for example, he got eighty in forty-five minutes if he went in at twelve and was out at twelve forty-five. Unless he bagged the bowling off the last ball of every over for the whole time of forty-five minutes, of course he got his eighty runs in much less than three-quarters of an hour.

I know that when I secured the quickest hundred prize in 1934 the time recorded was sixty-three minutes. But I am certain I never had anything like an hour's batting !

It is not possible, without an official time-keeper, to record regularly the time each batsman was *actually batting*, but it should be possible to make a note when, as often happens, a batsman is away from the ball for long spells at a time. I know I have many a time been for over a quarter of an hour a mere onlooker while my partner had all the amusement, but each such quarter of an hour has been included in the time it took me to make my runs.

One's actual time at the wicket is also sometimes occupied by other distractions than those concerning the clouting of a moving ball to some place where there is no fieldsman. I was involved once in the following sequence of incidents which, after I have described them, will probably look rather like an account of the break up of a Rugby scrum.

My partner played the ball in what I must state was a "needle" match at its most exciting stage on the third afternoon. He hit it between mid-on and short leg and called me. Directly I started the bowler ran across in an obvious attempt to hinder me. I managed to dodge round him and was carrying on when just as I saw the wicket-keeper advancing, elbows out, across my path, the bowler seized the waistband of my trousers, jerking me back. By the time he had done this mid-on had fielded the ball and thrown at the wicket towards which I was, at last, running unimpeded. The wicket was broken when I was yards away. On my appeal the umpire gave the only possible verdict :

"Not out—unfair play."

I went on to make a hundred, but we lost the match. Being unused to cricket under Rugby rules !

Rambling along these paths of Kentish memories, I find myself once more at the beloved Angel ground, Tonbridge, where, in the instance I am about to quote, I find an object lesson for any who may care to learn of the value of slow left-hand bowling after rain.

It was on the occasion of my first match against Warwickshire and that was in 1913, on June 19th, 20th, 21st. Mr. F. R. Foster won the toss and Warwickshire made 360, so that I regard my 16.5 overs, 4 maidens, 44 runs, 5 wickets, with some satisfaction as one of my best performances. It rained overnight and Kent were out for 170, to which I contributed 8. We began towards the end of our innings, we being "Charlie" Blythe and myself, to build castles through the windows of which we thought we saw Kent following on, making a good recovery, knocking the cover off Mr. Foster and all that kind of thing and setting them 160 or so to get ; we two getting our own back, and winning the match, on a cut-up surface in fourth innings.

"No fear," said Mr. Foster as he reached the pavilion, when some member asked if he was making us follow on. "We've got you where we want you, we're going in again, and you can have fourth innings on that stuff."

Fred Huish overheard this, and said to Mr. Foster :

"You know, I've seen sides out for next to nothing on such a pitch, with two left-handers bowling."

But the Warwickshire captain had made up his mind, so out we trooped for their second innings.

So did they, they trooped forwards and backwards for a spell of forty minutes. I regret to say I have not got Blythe's full analysis. Mine read:

| O | M | R | W |
|---|---|---|---|
| 5 | 1 | 8 | 5 |

and Warwickshire totted up 16 runs all told!

I know Blythe also had 5 for 8 runs. I made 76 not out in our second innings, and Kent won comfortably.

I always think of that experience when I read of captains taking the unjustifiable risk, *if they have not got at least one good slow left-hander in their team*, of putting the other side in on winning the toss.

Putting the others in when you can only bowl them off-break or ordinary-paced everyday kind of right-hander stuff is suicide.

That is so because that kind of bowling, coming on to the bat as it does, is much more easily dealt with by resolute or experienced batsmen than the same batsmen can deal with bowling which sends the ball, after pitching, *away from the bat*.

The only sound justification a captain has for putting the other side in after rain is when he knows his opponents to have perhaps a brace of slow left-handers who will get rid of his side more cheaply, while the wicket is doing something, than, so he estimates, his side with only one left-hander, or perhaps none, is likely to get rid of them.

Even then it is a sheer gamble.

Because, no matter how good the left-hander may be, nobody can accurately foretell either of two things: (1) how the wicket will really play, or how long its difficult period will last, and (2) how any given bowler will bowl under any given set of conditions.

Every bowler who is honest can tell you of his own

failures to get wickets when, before going on to bowl, he has himself thought that the conditions were ideal for him.    Every experienced cricketer will tell you of instances where his opinion of how the wicket will play after rain has been completely falsified when put to the proof.

Putting opponents in is, in my opinion, *always* a gamble.

Its chief, if not its only justification, is that it gives spectators something more to talk about, and the critics something more to write about.

Mr. Wyatt certainly did that last August.    He put South Africa in in fine weather on, to all appearances, a batsman's wicket.    That was not the first time in Test history a captain had put his opponents in in fine weather after a long spell of fine weather.    For that innovation we must go back just on a dozen years when H. W. Taylor put us in at Birmingham in 1924. I don't think he has forgotten the incident, for we made 438 and South Africa 30 and 390.

Mr. Wyatt's action was thoroughly justifiable last August when he gambled on a good start for his bowlers.

Supposing he had had a start such as Sid Barnes gave us at Melbourne in December, 1911, when he sent Bardsley, Kelleway, Hill, and Armstrong back for 10 runs between them on a perfect wicket, England might have saved the rubber last year.    Putting South Africa in after winning the toss was the only way to do that, short of going in to bat, long handling, and *everything coming off for England*.    It was not an occasion for the employment of normal tactics, therefore Mr. Wyatt was quite right to leave the beaten track to fish in an unknown pool.    Even at the risk of finding it untenanted.    I thought that much of the censure he received for taking the risk he did was quite undeserved.

Though I strongly support what Mr. Wyatt did then,

I as strongly advise taking first innings every time in our three-day cricket when you have the option.

Pitches are not always so bad as they may look, and the cricket-truth, that runs are in all circumstances easier to save than to make, has stood the test of time, remaining as true to-day as it was whenever it was coined.

I have already stated that the risk of putting the other in is unjustifiable if you have not at least one good slow left-handed bowler in your team.  To illustrate the devastation for which such a bowler can be responsible I will give the facts of "Charlie" Blythe's seventeen wickets in one day for Kent, before I declare my Kentish chapter closed.  I do not suppose cricket lovers are aware how near "Charlie" went, that memorable day in 1907 at Northampton, to taking all twenty ! A feat in first-class cricket still open to all-comers.  It has been done in club cricket.

Charlie took all ten in the first innings, and continued his capers by collectiong the first seven in their second innings without turning a hair and scarcely making a remark.  Mr. G. A. T. Vials, who was a very capable batsman, then came in low down for some reason or another.  He returned the first ball to him an absolute "sitter" to Blythe, who remembered everything except to catch it !

That catch held would have been 18 wickets, and two really prize rabbits—with all deference to our opponents—to come in.  Poor "Charlie" ! I think that miss so upset him he could not bowl another ball. After that they made about 36 more runs, and he did not get another wicket.

I do not think I can begin better to draw my Kentish innings in this book to a close than by mentioning that great feat of Kent's greatest bowler, and certainly one of her most delightful characters.  "Charlie" Blythe was a favourite wherever he went.  It says much for a bowler when his opponents were always glad to see

C

him even if there had been a thunderstorm overnight and "the middle" looked, therefore, a Blythe special.

Of the many splendid comrades I have had, and friends I have made in the Kent XI, I find it beyond me to write. Partly because we have been always such a happy family, and it is not part of my creed to lift the veil of an almost intimate life for the general gaze. Like every well-ordered family, we have had our tiffs, since the occupants of the dressing-room of our cricket pavilions are human even if they are cricketers. I would greatly envy any county which had a happier side than we of Kent have been during the thirty years I have had the honour of being one of the team. As I have written elsewhere, a defeat for Kent is not regarded by us as the end of the world, and we all know for sure that the right spirit of cricket has no place for a bad loser. I know we try to play up to that. I sincerely hope that Kentish cricket always will. In that I have the utmost confidence, for our tradition is very strong, and every one of our young professionals seems to know what is expected of him almost before he has played in his first match for us. For this happy state of affairs we have the late Lord Harris and a long succession of splendid captains as well as members of the Kent XI to thank.

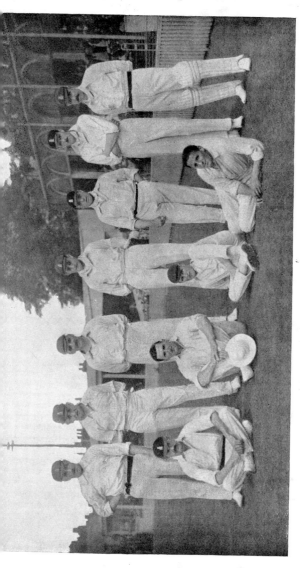

THE ENGLAND ELEVEN IN MY FIRST TEST, AT KENNINGTON OVAL,
AUGUST 9, 10, 11, 1909

W. Rhodes, Mr. D. W. Carr, Mr. A. C. MacLaren (capt.), Mr. R. H. Spooner, J. Sharp,
F. E. Woolley, A. A. Lilley

(Seated) E. G. Hayes, Mr. C. B. Fry, S. F. Barnes, Mr. K. L. Hutchings

Australia, 325 and 339 for 5 (dec.); England, 352 and 104 for 3. Drawn
Bardsley's 136 and 130 was the first instance of twins in a Test

I PREFER GOING IN FIRST

"He saw me go in first with Jack Hobbs at Lord's in June, 1930. . . ."

# CHAPTER III

ENGLAND did not engage in a Test Match with Australia or South Africa from August 9, 10, 11, 1909, at the Oval, against Australia, to August 14 to 18, 1926, also against Australia at the Oval, in which I did not play.

As I can almost hear the reader sigh as he says: "I hope he's not going through the lot ball by ball," I hasten to add that I am not cruel by nature.

I hope, therefore, my readers will bear with me while I wander along memory's avenues, stopping here and there only to write down such incidents as I can recall. For I never made any notes or, perhaps just as well, kept cuttings of matches. So, if I make a slip here or there, may I be excused. It is, after all, a cricketer's prerogative to give chances.

At the end of the book will be found the complete figures of my Test Match record, in the course of which it will be seen that only in two Tests, 1924 *v*. S. Africa at Old Trafford, and 1926 in the first Test at Nottingham against Australia, I did not bat; that I was run out four times; that I was lbw nine times; hit wicket twice, and stumped six times, in 98 ininngs in 64 Tests.

My first Test took place in brilliant August weather at the Oval in 1909. That was the season in which Jack Hobbs had started at Birmingham his brilliant Test Match career in the first of the series of five Tests. Mr. A. C. MacLaren, who was a great captain in every sense of the word, but not a lucky one, captained England in every Test of that year. After England had won the first Test easily by 10 wickets, M. A. Noble won the toss at Lord's and put England in, winning the game by 9 wickets, Vernon Ransford making 143 not out.

Australia won the next by 126 runs at Leeds, Charlie Macartney, 7 for 58 and 4 for 27, doing the winning.

The fourth Test at Manchester was drawn in Australia's favour after that clever right-hander Frank Laver had taken 8 for 31 in England's first innings of 119, and Barnes 5 for 56 and Blythe 5 for 63 had got Australia out for 147. They made 279 for 9 in their second innings, Rhodes 5 for 83, leaving England 308 to get. England had Messrs. Warner and Spooner and J. T. Tyldesley out for 108 at close of play.

So that Noble was one up when he won the toss in the fifth Test at the Oval. This being a three-day match, he was on velvet, as he had only to draw it to win the rubber.

The match was remarkable as being Trumper's last Test in England, and the first in which a hundred in each innings was made by the same player, Warren Bardsley making 136 and 130, and taking his time about it.

I remember that owing chiefly to the bowling of trial balls over a quarter of an hour elapsed between the fall of Rhodes' wicket—he made 66—and the bowling of the first ball to me. It was rather a trying time for me, especially as it was my first Test innings. In those days a bowler could go on at any time between the overs and bowl a few balls to loosen his muscles, but in 1910 the practice of bowling "trial" balls when two batsmen are at the wicket was made illegal. On the occasion I refer to some such balls went right down to the sight-screen, and, nobody going to fetch the ball, this had to be returned by a policeman or a spectator. I cannot help thinking this waste of time gave birth to the alteration to Law 18 which abolished "trial" ball bowling when there are two batsmen at the wicket.

Thus it became no longer possible to get away with the impudent trick played in an up-country match in Australia in the early days by, they always say, an Englishman. This wideawake player was bowled all over his wicket first ball. "Ha !" said he laughing as he picked up and replaced the bails, "now let's get on with it ; I *never could play those darn trial balls.*"

After my long wait it is perhaps not surprising that "Tibs" Cotter bowled me for 8. Cotter was a really fast right-hander with a long, swinging, rather round-arm action. He could keep up his pace for a long time, mainly, I think, because of his easy action and strong back. He got 6 for 95 in that innings, Messrs. Spooner, MacLaren, and Hutchings among them. On that tour he took most wickets in the Tests with 17 for 21.47 each.

Throughout the tour Noble always began with a fast or fast-medium and a medium or slow bowler as his first pair, as did Mr. MacLaren, with, in turn, Hirst and Blythe (all twenty wickets in the first Test), Hirst and King, Hirst and Barnes, Hirst and Barnes, and Barnes and our Kent googlie bowler, Mr. D. W. Carr, then thirty-seven years old, and in his first first-class season and first Test match.

Mr. MacLaren baptized him thoroughly while about it, as his analyses show :—

| O | M | R | W |
|---|---|---|---|
| 34 | 2 | 146 | 5 |
| 35 | 1 | 136 | 2 |

That was not Trumper's introduction to googlies, because he had been opposed by Mr. B. J. T. Bosanquet in Australia in 1903–04, and again in England in 1905, but when he was stumped off Mr. Carr in the second innings of the 1909 match for 20, having made 73 in the first innings, it was the only time his wicket fell to a googlie bowler in Test cricket.

I know how deeply I was impressed with the fluency

of Trumper's strokes, and with the way he made runs off good-length balls.

Jack Sharp, who is one of the cheeriest Lancastrians I ever met, was played for England in my first Test for his fast bowling. But Mr. MacLaren, who had the choice between him and Buckenham, of Essex, had other ideas. If he did not know his countyman's form, who, indeed, should ? So Sharp bowled only 16·3 overs in the first and 12 in the second innings, but he was sent in third wicket down and made 105. How sound was Mr. MacLaren's estimate of Sharp's capabilities is proved by the fact that while he took 3 wickets for 37 runs each in the three Tests he played in, he finished first in the averages with an average of 47.

It is worth while mentioning here that that year, 1909, England called upon 25 players in the five Tests, as compared to 30 in the researches for Test class players during the 1921 Australian tour here ; 21 in 1930 ; and only 18 in 1934. I think that selection committees are not always fairly criticized in this matter of numbers of players they call upon. Like most such complaints, this one will not bear examination. It is usually advanced against them that a large number shows indecision on their part, and inability of knowing their own minds. I cannot follow that line of reasoning, or subscribe to it as justifiable criticism.

Though we lost the rubber with 18 different players in 1934, England won it in 1905, having called on 19 !

Though England played only three Tests, and those the less exacting three-day affairs, in 1912, yet she called on 14 men before she could win one Test of the three played against Australia. In the same season 15 were needed with whom to defeat South Africa three times in three games. The calling upon a large number of players is the very last thing any Selection Committee would do *unless compelled to do so* by the proved inadequacy of certain players themselves. The fact that they have done so is certainly no proof that the selectors don't know their own minds.

In those days South Africa was very strong, with such as G. A. Faulkner, H. W. Taylor, A. D. Nourse, sen., S. J. Pegler (a grand bowler, this one), R. O. Schwarz, past his best, L. J. Tancred, and C. B. Llewellyn, the first bowler of left-hand googlies.

With which type of bowling I am much mistaken if the Australian, L. O'B. Fleetwood-Smith, does not make a big mark on the pages of cricket during the coming few seasons.

In that year England had one of the best captains in my time, Mr. C. B. Fry. He was a great batsman, one of the very few right up at the top *who really knew how to bat* for the particular wicket against the bowlers then engaged. He would not use the same methods against every bowler, and on soft or difficult wickets nobody in my experience moved his right foot farther back than Mr. Fry did as a habit. I question whether he was ever out "hit wicket" in spite of the full use he made of his ground.

My next experiences of Test cricket came when I played in every Test of the M.C.C. South African tour of 1909–10, under surely the cheeriest captian ever a team could wish for, Mr. H. D. G. Leveson-Gower. The one cricketer who I have never seen with other but a smiling face, and who, to use one of his pet phrases, was always "pale but confident." I do not wonder that his intimate friends nicknamed him "the Shrimp." I know I have often with difficulty restrained myself from calling him that, and I feel that he would have pardoned me had I so ventured. To say that he was the life and soul of our happy band is to put the matter mildly indeed.

Mr. Leveson-Gower was one of those class cricketers whose value to his side it is quite impossible to assess by a glance at his figures. For he was a good batsman, one of the very best at a pinch, and quite irrespective of who was bowling. I call him a really good judge of a cricketer, and a most excellent captain. Up to every move on the board, he was one of the finest handlers of his bowling I ever saw.

The way he used Mr. Simpson-Hayward's lobs on that tour was masterly. While G. J. Thompson got 23 wickets for 26·9 runs each in 223 overs, and Buckenham 21 wickets for 28·2 runs each in 197 overs, our "lobster" took 23 wickets for 18.2 runs each, 6 apiece less than Thompson, in only 149 overs. But for our captain's careful nursing of this finger-flick bowler we should have lost the rubber by more than three defeats to two wins. I feel confident about that.

"Charlie" Blythe had one great match, the fifth Test at Cape Town, where the wicket was of matting over turf. He took 7 for 46 and 3 for 30, and we won by 9 wickets. I had a bad match, getting a duck, and taking 3 for 47 in the second innings after not bowling in the first. This disappointed me, as in the fourth Test on the same ground the previous week I made 69 and 64, after 58 not out and none in the previous one on the hard-as-iron matting over red rubble wicket at the Wanderers' ground, Johannesburg. In the first two Tests I had done moderately with 14 and 25, and 22 and 4, respectively, and having little bowling to do. I held a catch in every Test, four in the third.

Jack Hobbs was with us, easily heading the averages with 67.37, and an aggregate of 539. I was third with 256, an average of 32. Jack fairly mastered the googlie on that trip, on which Vogler, 224 overs for 36 wickets at 21·7 apiece, and G. A. Faulkner, 209 for 29 wickets at 21·8 each, were the only two South Africans to bowl more than 52 overs. The next highest bag of wickets by a South African were the 4 each taken by N. O. Norton, fast right ; A. D. Nourse, medium left ; S. J. Snooke, fast right ; and J. H. Sinclair, medium right. R. O. Schwarz, who had been such a success on the 1907 tour in England, bowled only 8 overs in the series, for no wickets. I cannot account for such a sudden loss of form on the part of so fine a cricketer.

I do not suppose I shall ever forget an umpiring incident of that tour. A clearer proof that umpires are only human, after all, I never saw. It happened in a game at Queenstown. A youngster had batted well enough to get into the eighties when Buckenham was put on. Soon the boy had a welt at an off ball, there was the noise of a snick, and we all joined in the chorus when Strudwick shouted : "How's that ?"

To our amazement the umpire replied : "Not out."

Seeing that the youngster was out of his ground, "Struddy" had a shy at the wicket, missed it, and the ball went to the boundary. The scorer now took a hand in the game.

"Was that a hit, or are those byes ?" he shouted.

Without hesitation : "Hit," roared the umpire.

You see, he was the batsman's father !

Somehow Queenstown seems to have been for me a sort of amusement depot on that tour. In another game there we lost the toss, and, getting on to the wicket, began to bowl trial balls. We all seemed to be bowling frightfully short, so we asked the grounds-man about the length of the wicket. "I measured it myself," said he. "*Thirty*-two yards !"

That, of course, had to be put right, so fresh creases were marked. Soon after we had begun playing, Mr. Leveson-Gower was called away to meet the Mayor of the town, who had just arrived.

This was a situation that suited "Charlie" Blythe down to the ground. "Got any three-inch nails ?" said he to the groundsman. These were soon forthcoming, and, under "Charlie's" direction, several were pegged down just about the leg-stump blind spot. Nothing was said, and, as luck would have it, when Mr. Leveson-Gower came bustling back, with his elbows out, full

c*

of pep to get the game alive again, he must needs trip up on these nails. The fat was in the fire now. He sent for the groundsman, and just as that sportsman looked like being for the carpet, "Charlie" owned up, and in due course all was well.

When I think of that harmless bit of fun now I cannot help wondering if such a thing happened in these days whether the cables would be set a-clicking and M.C.C. be asked to recall the player responsible. And I ask, who was one penny the worse for this little bit of by-play ?

It was on that 1909–10 tour that I was concerned in the most astonishing case of attempted umpiring—I really cannot call it umpiring—in the whole of my experience. It is not, and, I am proud to say, never has been, part of my cricket to question the umpire's decision. I believe this is generally regarded as an outstanding trait in the Kentish cricket character, and I say it, knowing that what I say is literally true, that the Kent Eleven never had any use for a grouser. From our nursery days we are made to understand that wrong decisions are as much part of the game of cricket as are the implements without which we cannot play it. I believe my county's eleven has always borne a sweet reputation in this respect, and I feel sure that those who carry on the torch will see to it that this characteristic will never change.

So that what I have to say now must not be taken as a wholesale condemnation of umpiring in South Africa, which, in my experience, has been neither better nor worse than I found it to be elsewhere.

On the occasion of which I now write seven of us were given out lbw. I can vouch for two of the seven not having been out.

Mr. Leveson-Gower, standing upright while attempting his stroke, was hit under the armpit, and not by a full toss.

I was bowled a full pitch which I hit to the square

leg boundary (the ball never having touched me at all), but was given out lbw, as was my captain.

I think I am justified in objecting to both those two decisions, let alone the other five, and in stating that the umpire, as in the Queenstown incident, was the father of the bowler, who was bowling for a club that had never beaten a touring English side.

They won that time.

My first tour in Australia, 1911–12, under the captaincy of that great enthusiast, Mr. P. F. Warner, followed my first South African tour. Owing to Mr. Warner's unfortunate illness, the late Mr. J. W. H. T. Douglas captained in all five Tests, of which we—or I should say Mr. F. R. Foster and Barnes—won four, Australia one.

I have written fully about these two bowlers and the events of that tour in another chapter. They were the most destructive pair on hard wickets I ever saw, whether for England or any other country.

Australian cricket was just then at the parting of the ways. Formerly the players had chosen the teams that visited England and had made their own sharing-out arrangements. Now the management of the game is vested in their Board of Control, a body which had been unfortunate never to have enough former Test or State cricketers serving on it.

The only people who can really govern and control big cricket are those who have played in it, and who therefore understand it from the centre, not from the outskirts of the ground.

In other words, in my opinion, Wicket Knowledge is absolutely essential in a cricket councillor or legislator.

Cricket cannot be governed on hearsay.

From all one hears and reads, Australian cricket has been less happy since the days before the Board took control. We in England are in much better case. It is not for me to criticize authority, but, whether our Board makes mistakes or not, I have never heard a cricketer make a better suggestion for running our cricket than the existing one.

It was on the 1911–12 tour that I made my acquaintance with the famous shirt-front wickets which Australia boasted in those days. Since then wicket conditions out there have changed, so I am told, and the Sydney Oval wicket is not now quite of the kind upon which, as Mr. A. C. MacLaren is reputed with saying, "You've only to put out your tongue and it's a four." Most of the Australian wickets were then made of Bulli soil, and the result sometimes almost shone. A ball made of this particular kind of clay is in the pavilion at Lord's as a kind of curiosity. It resembles a cannon ball. Although in fine weather this stuff produced a pitch that made a bowler bowl for his wickets, to put it mildly, it needed knowing after rain. Here in England we used to get a "sticky dog" now and then, but always fairly slow paced. Out there after rain, and especially at Melbourne, the pitch becomes a fast "sticky dog" for about a couple of hours. A thing indescribable. It must be experienced.

In my time, and this characteristic may still exist at Sydney, so I mention it for the benefit of our next Hopes, the wicket there got dusty in fine weather by the third day. This had the curious result of causing a tendency to make the ball shoot.

I discovered this on my 1920–21 tour while watching Charlie Macartney.

In his first innings he risked a cross-bat stroke more than once, but after the third day his blade was rigidly up and down the wicket on the flight of the ball. He told me, on my asking him about the very noticeable difference in his methods, that he had to do this because of the possibility of shooters.

It was on my 1911–12 tour I first encountered Dr. H. V. Hordern. In my judgment he will always be the best of the googlie bowlers, because of his extra pace compared to all the others, with his perfect length. In which latter respect Clarrie Grimmett was his equal. Though when I was first opposed by Clarrie on the 1924–5 tour's Fifth Test he was a different bowler from the one we have seen on the last two tours here. He always had length and his own curved flight. Quite different from the curve, either inwards or outwards, which is usually understood when curve or swerve is mentioned.

Grimmett's bowling, owing to the height of his hand at the release, curved upwards and then downwards. In addition, when the wind was blowing suitably from third-man (for a right-handed batsman, or, as in my case, from long-leg) his bowling made the ball "drift," rather than swerve, away from me, but *into* a right-hander. Right-handers are often l.b.w. to Grimmett. Not under the 1935 rule—under which conditions Grimmett has not yet bowled in a first-class match as I write this.

I was never l.b.w. to him, but I was twice stumped off him—through missing the "drifter"—and once hit wicket to him in Test cricket.

I embarked Grimmett on his magnificently successful Test career, as in the fifth Test of the 1925–6 tour mine was the first wicket he took in that his first Test. I must have brought him luck, as his first two analyses read :—

| O | M | R | W |
|------|---|----|---|
| 11.7 | 2 | 45 | 5 |
| 20 | 3 | 35 | 6 |

Which, when it is remembered that our team included Jack Hobbs (1), Sutcliffe, Sandham (1), Hendren (1), Jack Hearne (2), Whysall (2), Roy Kilner (1), is one of the greatest bowling feats in the history of Test cricket for a first appearance. The figures in brackets denote the times Grimmett got the wicket of the player named. The "drifter" got Sandham and Jack Hearne each time, and Whysall once.

My first tour in Australia was hall-marked for me by the fact that during its course I made my only score of over 300 runs. Concerning which there is a rather amusing story. I do not know if all the young professionals of to-day would stand, or have any experience of, the severe schooling which young professionals had in my early days. It has to be remembered that I had played for England six times before I went on that tour to Australia and had averaged 32 for Kent in a full season's cricket.

But, in Australia, I was almost invariably number eight or nine in the batting order!

The climax appeared to have arrived when in a game like that at Hobart against Tasmania I found myself at number nine! As I was on the tour at all more for my batting than for anything else I could not understand this. But Sid Barnes, who was always a good pal to me, knew the solution!

"Look here, Frank," said he, "you get your pads on and hang around the dressing room. Never mind about number nine because I've a sort of notion that Phil Mead will be missing when the second wicket falls."

I must say here that Mr. Douglas, who captained during Mr. Warner's illness, did not cross over to Tasmania with us so Mr. F. R. Foster was captain.

When the second wicket fell no Phil Mead could be found!

So out I hustled, not daring to look at my captain's face, and for the time being deaf to the world.

My chief recollection of that innings is Mr. Foster signalling to me to have a dip after I had got my century. So I did. I dipped several times, had quite a decent swim in fact—305 not out in under five hours.

For the rest of the trip, however, I was at number seven and nine in the batting order. It was a different world then.

One more reminiscence of Tasmania. As all who

have never been there cannot know the sea crossing is almost always a "beast." I suppose it was a ship we crossed in, but hardened travellers would soon have found another word for it. It was a filthy dark night, and there was an unfortunate passenger huddled on a bench at the side, engaged at intervals as is customary on such occasions. Even the captain could not stand it, so he came down from the bridge and, patting the man on the shoulder, said :

"Cheer up, son, you'll soon be all right ; the moon comes up in a few minutes and then the sea'll go down."

I can hear the groan now as the hapless traveller replied : "Good —— ! Has *that* got to come up, too ?"

After this tour I had a spell of South African cricket in the Triangular tournament in 1912 here, where I crossed bats with that grand right-handed off-break bowler, Sid Pegler, and in 1913–14 in South Africa. A strong, tall man, Pegler bowled what were leg breaks to right-handers, at a fair pace with splendid precision. In the June Test at Lord's against England Pegler accomplished one of the most memorable bowling feats in all Test history. England had a very strong batting side, which went in this order :

Hobbs, Rhodes, Mr. R. H. Spooner, Commander C. B. Fry, Mr. P. F. Warner, Woolley, Mr. G. L. Jessop, Mr. F. R. Foster, Smith (E. J.), Barnes, Mr. W. Brearley.

We had 308 on the board for four and Mr. Warner and I were in.

We were all out for 337 !

On going on for the first time at the pavilion end seven runs were hit off Pegler's first over, and he then took the next six wickets for nine runs. I was the first to go, clean bowled for 73. Mr. Jessop made three and suffered the same fate, then Mr. Warner was stumped and Mr. Foster l.b.w.

It was a great bit of bowling, which illustrated the wisdom of a captain never being satisfied with keeping

one of his best bowlers always on from only one end.
It is a very old, and as I see it a baseless, theory that
a leg-break bowler can only bowl from the nursery end
at Lord's. That is just as groundless as is that other
one that only the pavilion end there suits a fast bowler.

I can assure anybody who places faith in that fallacy
that had he batted in the 1921 Australian Test at
Lord's, with Gregory and Macdonald bowling, he
would have had stinging reasons for changing his creed.

M.C.C. sent a very strong team to South Africa in
1913–14 under Lord Tennyson and we had little difficulty in winning four out of five Tests, the first two
by an innings, the fifth by ten wickets, the third by
91 runs, and drawing the fourth, the only one in which
we were at all held. South Africa made 170 and 305
for 9, England 163 and 154 for 5. Hearne and I were
not out, with Mr. Morice Bird, Relf (A. E.), Barnes
and Strudwick to come.

Barnes had a great tour. They couldn't look at
him, excepting always H. W. Taylor, who confirmed
his 1912 England form with this sequence : 109, 8, 29,
40, 14, 70, 16, 93, 42, 87, an aggregate of 508 and
average of 50.80. Barnes had 49 for 10.93 as his Test
figures. In the second Test, on matting over rubble,
his figures were :

| O | M | R | W |
|---|---|---|---|
| 26.5 | 9 | 56 | 8 |
| 38.4 | 7 | 103 | 9 |

Barnes played in only four Tests, and his sequence
of wickets was 10, 17, 8 and 14. After which, South
Africa heaved a sigh of relief when he could not play
at Port Elizabeth in the fifth Test—but they lost it all
the same. Strudwick was in grand form throughout
this tour.

Hobbs, Rhodes, Mead, Hearne, Lord Tennyson, Mr.
Bird and Mr. Douglas formed too much of a nucleus
of batsmen, with Barnes, Relf, M. W. Booth (of York-

shire) to follow for South Africa, who were then
without Vogler, Schwarz and Sinclair, and with nobody
of their class to replace them.

Nor has South Africa ever since been as strong as
she was in 1907 when G. A. Faulkner was at his best,
and Vogler, Schwarz, G. C. White, J. H. Sinclair,
S. J. Snooke, P. W. Sherwell, L. J. Tancred and
A. D. Nourse were at their zenith.

Since 1907 the only three cricketers South Africa
has produced in their own 1907 class are H. W. Taylor,
Bruce Mitchell and H. B. Cameron.

When I encountered South Africa again in the Tests
of 1922–3 out there, and again against their weak side
of 1924 here, their cricket was poor by comparison
with their magnificent 1907 team against which I
played at Catford Bridge, to be caught by Faulkner
in both innings, off Schwarz in the first and White in
the second.

Schwarz was a great off-break bowler. It was in
the very early days of my career when I opposed
him and I have met since a good many bowlers of the
off-break but none to equal him at making the ball
turn from the off on a good wicket. He did it with the
googlie action but he did not vary his attack by
bowling the true leg-break.

It was on the 1922–23 tour I first encountered the
one-eyed Swede, E. A. Nupen. A good bowler on
matting was this one, but most strangely ineffective
on turf. So different from our Sid Barnes, who could
bowl on anything. South Africa thought a lot of
Nupen, as they did of J. M. Blanckenberg, but neither
did much in England.

I never think of the next South African team to
visit us, that of 1924, without recalling a very funny
incident in the first Test at Birmingham. The year
before Kent had played a couple of games in Scotland,
where we ran up against a fast bowler named Parker.
While I was batting he, who happened to be bowling,

asked me to place his field for him, which I did ! The
next time I saw him I was batting in the first Test of
1924, when he came up to me and said : "My field
placed all right, Frank ?" So he had not forgotten.

A little later on when it was his turn to begin an
over, Parker put the ball down and, without saying a
word to a soul, walked down the wicket and straight
into the pavilion ! Somebody went after him and we
heard afterwards that all he said was : "I'm simply
whacked, I can't bowl another ball."

South Africa had brought him into the side at the
eleventh hour, as they were hard up for bowling and he
was not a member of the touring side. That day
Taylor had put us in on a plumb 'un and we had
given their bowling a rare dusting. Parker was not in
training, with one-day cricket, for the severe calls of
Test cricket.

Against the 1924 team I made 134 not out in the
second Test at Lord's, after 64 in that first one at
Birmingham, but Pegler bowled me before I had
scored in the third Test at Leeds. I did not bat in the
fourth, but followed up 51 in the fifth at the Oval with
176 runs at Canterbury.

When the South Africans were here in 1929 I did
not play in the first two Tests, but made 83 and 95
not out in the third, 154 in the fourth, 46 in the fifth,
and finished up with 50 and 49 not out at Canterbury
and 111 at Folkestone against them, an aggregate of
588 for 5 innings, average 117.6.

Against the 1924 South African team my scores
were 64, 134 not out, 0, 51, 176, 4 and 26, total 455
for 6 innings, average 75.83.

If I had to choose the best South African eleven
from the men I played against it would contain two
wicket-keepers, either of whom could have been chosen
for his batting, in P. W. Sherwell and the late H. B.
Cameron. It would bat in this order : H. W. Taylor,
Bruce Mitchell, A. D. Nourse, senior, G. A. Faulkner,

G. C. White, H. B. Cameron, P. W. Sherwell, J. H. Sinclair, A. E. Vogler, S. J. Pegler and J. J. Kotze. Twelfth man, J. W. Zulch, junior. Every one of these is, or was, a Test class cricketer.

Few, if any, Test elevens anywhere in my time, except those containing Mr. F. R. Foster and Barnes, had as strong bowling as this South African one with Kotze, Vogler, Pegler, Faulkner, White and Sinclair, and nine of the side have made centuries in first-class cricket.

I always thoroughly enjoyed playing against South African teams. They play the game hard enough in all conscience, but, if I may say so without offending my Australian friends, they play it in a much cheerier, less business-like, way than do Australians.

I have also the most pleasurable recollections of playing against New Zealand teams, both here and in their most beautiful country on the tour of 1929–30 ; a country so lovely that in places it almost equalled my Kent !

The New Zealanders play cricket much as do the South Africans. Their geysers and hot springs do not explode if New Zealand loses, and they can win just as cheerfully as we can, with a handshake for the losers. The real blood of cricket courses through the veins of New Zealanders. I played, among other places, at Wellington, Otago, Ranjituku—they ought to breed batsmen there !—Christchurch, Dunedin, where I made 132, with my only other century on that tour, 125, at Manawatu. Everywhere enjoyable and happy though quite serious play, and open-handed hospitality. The wickets were up to standard, and for a country so young in first-class cricket the umpiring was excellent. These men are saturated in sport, they are natural Games-Men.

# CHAPTER IV

## MORE TEST REMINISCENCES

THERE is no doubt that Australian cricketers not only approach Test cricket in a different spirit from that in which we do, but they play in it differently.

That is apparent nowhere else, perhaps, so clearly as in captaincy, and in the manner wherein, after having got to three figures, their best batsmen continue as though "that is that, now for the second hundred" is a law of the game.

I cannot say I blame them, the object of the game being to make as many runs as possible. I wish we had a bit more of the same thoroughness. But as all our cricket at home is time-limited and theirs goes on for ever and ever they acquire the habit from their earliest days, while we, subconsciously perhaps, never even think of that second hundred until we suddenly find we have, perhaps, topped the 150, and then, and not before, begin to think we may as well have a go for it.

I have several times seen Australian batsmen on their century being signalled go on with their innings just as though they had just begun it, and bat as though they had still to reach double figures. It cannot be open to doubt which is the better paying method in matches in Australia.

Another factor which acts against the acquisition of this habit by English batsmen as compared to Australian is that of climate. Out in Australia the weather is either set fair or it is not. You do get a game now and then during which the players are hopping in and out of the pavilion on several occasions for a day or so, but such a thing is rare. Here we are inured to it, so that we get into a habit of either getting "on with it" in order to have runs to play with or, worse luck, of going to the other extreme and batting to not get out on any account. Thus bringing about the abortive drawn match, which is only worth noticing because your side has not lost.

An Australian batsman with, say, 105, against his name, time 2.30 on a brilliant Monday afternoon and only two wickets down, in a time-limitless match at Sydney, is in totally different case to that of an English batsman at the same time on the second afternoon of a three-day county match, perhaps at Old Trafford with a sou'-wester in the air. The Australian knows that if the other end stays there he may perhaps be still batting on Wednesday evening. He knows, too, that most of the other end *can* stay there, if they make up their mind to hold the bat straight to the straight ones and ignore the others. So he just pitches camp and looks about for food. This becomes a habit, and thus we get the Ponsford-Bradman type which, having got to say 150 in a Test over here, continue with cucumber cool brows to go on batting as though nothing had happened or, more important still, as though nothing really was happening. The fact that the flower of England's bowling is plugging away at them for all it is worth scarcely seems to occur to them when they are in this mood. They assume the air of an elephant being peppered with a pea-shooter, and our faithful public, naturally rather upset at the sight, goes home and writes to its pet Editor to tell him that our selectors have chosen the wrong bowlers, and that if they didn't know they should have known that Mr. So-and-so hasn't a captain's temperament.

I never ponder over this characteristic imperturbability of the Australian batsman without recalling the remark of honest "Struddy" in that Test at Adelaide, in 1921, when England found Charlie

Kelleway had taken root. Kelleway made 147 before a ball from Harry Howell contrived to get past his bat. He was at the wicket the greater part of three whole days !

On coming in on the third morning, with his score just over the hundred, if my memory serves, Kelleway said, "Good morning, Bert," as he arrived at "Struddy's" end, and began to take guard preparatory to going on, as we feared, for a day or two more.

"Hm !" snorted "Struddy" in feigned disgust, "I've been saying 'Good evening' and 'Good morning' to you for about a week, and I look like going on for a week more—blowed if I'm going to say 'Good morning' to-day—get on with the game !"

The lives of those of us who dwell in the slips is not all split fingernails and stingers on the wrists or the shins. We do get a laugh in now and then, and this was one such joyous occasion.

It was at Adelaide that happened on the tour of 1925, when Australia won by eleven runs, the cutest —certainly I do not call it the sharpest—bit of captaincy in my experience. There is no doubt that it helped Australia to win, and to that I will add the statement that if it is not a captain's duty to help his side whose duty is it ?

The match's course had so run that we had to make 375 to win in the fourth innings. We had made over 275 for 6 wickets when slight rain interrupted the game upon what looked like being the last day's play in any case.

Adelaide's wicket is notoriously one of the quickest drying ones.

The Australian bowlers, especially Gregory and Mailey, their two best, had had a pretty good doing, so that every quarter of an hour's rest they could get was well wanted by them, and of not much use to us. Soon after the rain stopped "Horseshoe" Collins took Mr. Gilligan *and the umpires* out with him to have a look at things, when it was perfectly obvious that such a light rain could hardly have made any difference to a pitch so hard and dry that close on 1,400 runs had been scored on it for 36 wickets.

The following is the gist of the conversation that took place alongside the wicket.

Said Collins to one of the umpires: "Looks to me, ——, as though we could play again in about an hour?"

"Yes, certainly," replied the umpire.

"Will that suit you, Arthur?" said Collins to Mr. Gilligan.

"Yes, I think so," replied our skipper.

The result was that the game was held up unnecessarily for a whole hour, which gave the bowlers very much needed rest, tended to break the grip we had on the game and, in my opinion, went far towards winning it.

There had been no previous disagreement between the captains to in any way justify Collins' leading question to the umpire, which put the idea of an hour's delay into both umpire's heads.

In the M.C.C.'s valuable Instructions to Umpires it is laid down that "as soon as rain has ceased the umpires shall immediately without further instruction inspect the wicket, unaccompanied by any of the players, etc., etc."

Test cricket everywhere is played under those Instructions, which are based on Law 43: "The umpires are sole judges of . . . the fitness of the ground, etc.," but the only place in which our Board of Control for Test matches at Home refers to the M.C.C.'s Instructions to Umpires is in their own Rule 26, and the reference there concerns only the mowing of the grass on the ground and on the wicket during a Test.

Although, however, Australian cricketers appear to have what is known as a bit of a nerve, we do get them rattled or on the run sometimes. One of the most remarkable instances of this in my experience happened at Sydney in December, 1924, and the reader will smile when I say who it was that put them at sixes and sevens. Nobody bigger than "Tich" Freeman as a batsman !

"Tich" came in eighth wicket down when I had made about fifty. As he passed me he said : "Suppose we'd better give 'em a bit of Kentish fire."

So I said : "All right, we'll make 'em get us out."

I have never seen "Tich" bat anything like he did that day. Mailey had got Hobbs, Sutcliffe and Sandham's wickets, and Gregory had bowled Hearne. Kelleway had taken two wickets. Sutcliffe, by the way, had made the first of his three successive hundreds in Test innings, 115, 176 and 127. H. L. Hendry had got two wickets and eventually ended the innings, in which England made over 400 in the fourth innings of a Test, a rare enough feat at any time.

"Tich" set about Gregory as though he was a medium-paced club bowler. Mailey he got into such a tangle that I can still hear Mailey saying to Collins : "I don't feel like getting Freeman out any way !"

It was during our partnership that the Australians actually talked about playing on another hour in order to finish the game that evening, which was the sixth evening of the match. But "Tich" and I had other ideas about this. We took them over into the seventh day, and it was not until nearly lunch time that Bert Strudwick was out caught at the wicket off Hendry, leaving "Tich" 50 not out.

I had a bit of water on the knee and could really do not much better than hobble. This may have proved a blessing in disguise and haved caused me to put the brake on a bit, for I had made 123 before I mistimed Gregory, to be caught by Mailey. I have the most distinct recollection of the closing stages of that innings having shown a jolly well rattled Australian side. And for that the grit and nerve of "Tich" was mainly responsible.

That was not my highest score in a Test, as I had made 133 not out in the first Test of the 1912 tour, also at Sydney. No wonder, perhaps, that I consider Sydney the best run-getting wicket in the world. Here are my consecutive scores there for all matches :

    1911—43 not out, 39, 7.
    1912—3, 133 not out, 11.
    1920—11, 26, 64 (retired), 52, 16, 20, 138, 53, 1.
    1924—0, 123, 149, 80, 47, 28.
    1929—219.

This gives me an average of 61 on Sydney with an aggregate of 1,163 for 19 innings. Or, if the "retired" counts as an innings, an average of 58.

While on the subject I give the first ten grounds in the order of merit from the batsman's point of view as I have found them : Sydney Oval, Kennington Oval, Canterbury, Worcester, Leyton, Southampton, Taunton, Cardiff, Bradford, Old Trafford.

I knew Kennington Oval in Sam Apted's time, and am not surprised that when the Marylebone Cricket Club decided to call in outside help last autumn in order to try to counteract the ravages of the Daddy Long Legs insect they decided on Apted's successor, my friend Martin, of the Oval.

That 1924 tour was memorable for the smashing performances of Sutcliffe, who made a hundred in his first Test innings, as well as a hundred in both of his first two Test matches, a feat which he shares with Bill Ponsford, who did the same thing on this tour. Sutcliffe, with a total of 734 for the five Tests (nine innings and an average of 81.5, was believed to have created a record that would stand for a very long time.

The eight-ball over was in vogue on this tour for the only time English bowlers have had to put up with this absurdity. The bowling analyses on both sides reflected how this innovation helps scoring. Mailey took 24 wickets for 41.02, Gregory 22 for 37.09 each. Tate had his Test record of 38 wickets for 23.18 each, grand figures, the late Roy Kilner next best with 17 for 23.47, Hearne 11 for 44.4, Mr. Gilligan 10 for 56.9, down to Mr. Douglas 1 for 104 each !

Sutcliffe's 734 was, however, not destined to remain long on the records, as four years later Wally Hammond sent it sky-high with 905 and an average of 113.12 in the five Tests of 1928–29, only to have to play second fiddle himself a year later.

Then, on our wickets, Don Bradman amazed the cricket world with an aggregate of 974 and an average of 139.14, which will, I hope, remain the record for five Test matches for ever.

In that year Bradman scored 131 in the first Test at Nottingham ; 254 in the second at Lord's ; 334 in the third at Leeds ; got a mud wicket to play on in the fourth at Manchester and made 14 ; to finish with a score of 232 in the fifth at the Oval. He was then given out to a catch at the wicket, not having played the ball, or would certainly have made an over 1,000 runs total for five Tests.

Hammond's batting on that 1928–29 tour was something, they tell me, which had to be seen to be believed. While in 1924–25 Sutcliffe made three successive centuries in the Tests, Hammond made two successive scores of 200, his complete nine innings reading : 44, 28, 251, 200, 32, 119 not out, 177, 38 and 16. His 779 total for four innings in the second, third and fourth Tests of that tour beats Bradman's 719 in the first, second and third Tests of 1930 in three innings.

It is generally the case when these most unusual individual scoring feats are accomplished that there is something of an outcry against the perfect condition of wickets. Is not some of this often-heard objection unreasonable ? If not, how is it that such high scoring

only occurs very rarely, and is nearly always the work
of only one individual ?

Are all the contemporaries of Bradman and Hammond then such incompetent batsmen ?  They play
under exactly similar conditions as Bradman and
Hammond, but do not produce results approaching
those of these two at their best.  So how can the blame
for such tall scoring be placed at the door of the
preparers of the wicket ?

If blame must be apportioned—and for my part I
really cannot see that the public ought to have anything but praise for the good fortune which gives them
the sight of such players as Bradman and Hammond
in form—it should be addressed to the fieldsmen who
drop the catches, the bowlers who cannot hit the
wicket, and the captain who, perhaps, by not placing
his field in the right place helps such prolific stroke-
players to make such big scores.  They are, between
them, far more to blame than are the wickets.

As a special example.  There was a memorable
occasion when Charlie Macartney scored a century
before lunch in the Test match at Leeds in 1926, on
a good wicket.  Competent judges of long experience
both of playing in and of watching Test match cricket
say that that innings was the greatest ever played in
Test cricket, at any rate in their experience.  It was certainly one of the most exhilarating in any Test I played
in.  Macartney was missed when he had made two runs.

Now, which do the objectors to the over-preparation
of wickets "blame" for that score, the super-excellence
of the pitch, the ability of the batsman, or the catch
missed at third slip by Mr. A. W. Carr, baulked by
George Geary's movement from second slip ?

Personally I *blame* nobody for a display which gave
so much pleasure to "old hands."  I give the fullest
credit, unstinted, to the man who made the runs.

I think people who scatter blame so freely because
the ground is properly got ready for first-class cricket

to be played on forget that there are nine ways, plus an umpire's natural proneness to err, by which a batsman can lose his wicket, and that bowlers can get wickets, quite irrespective of how perfect the pitch may be, by (a) flight, and by (b) not bowling the same stuff to each successive batsman, as though every batsman is a mere Robot who bats the same way as his predecessor.

That is the other side of the picture which grumblers may not care to look at because it is easier to just say that the wickets are too good nowadays and leave it at that.

For myself, going back over thirty years, the only difference I see in the pitches is that we rarely get now a "sticky dog" of quite the vicious nature of my early days such as, for example, that one at Kennington Oval in 1912 when Sid Barnes took 13 South African wickets for 56 runs. As I took 5 for 41 and 1 for 21 and bowled 24 overs on it I write from knowledge. It was far the most difficult wicket at the Oval in my experience—Sam Apted had prepared it.

I may mention here that that was a pretty bad August. That match was played on August 12th and 13th, and on August 19th to 22nd we got another bad wicket at the Oval, but nothing like the first one, when playing the Australians.

Perhaps the spirit of the famous old Kent left-hander, "Nutty" Martin, was hovering about at that match, for I got these analyses :

| O | M | R | W |
|---|---|---|---|
| 9.4 | 3 | 29 | 5 |
| 7.4 | 1 | 20 | 5 |

Twenty-two years previously in the days of five-ball overs "Nutty's" figures against Australia at the Oval were :

| O | M | R | W |
|---|---|---|---|
| 27 | 9 | 50 | 6 |
| 30.2 | 12 | 52 | 6 |

Of the twenty-four cases of bowlers who have taken ten wickets or more in a Test against Australia (ten cases by left-handers), I am proud to say that my 10 for 49 is numerically the best performance. M. A. Noble's 13 for 77 at Melbourne in 1902 is next best.

I think that the profession of groundsman has discovered some means whereby dry wickets have less "life" than they used to have before the War, but otherwise the wickets in general are little or no better than those of pre-War, except at Lord's where, excepting of course the unusual conditions of 1935, the pitch has become tame out of recognition with what it was twenty-five years ago.

The England side which played against the returned M.C.C. Australian team of 1911–12 at Lord's in May 1912, and had then to cope with Mr. Foster and Sid Barnes on one that "flew a bit," would think they were in another world if they could have had a replay on the same ground in 1934 before the Daddy Long Legs chose to camp there.

The over-prepared wicket is too easy an excuse for incompetent bowling to be the true cause of tall scoring.

A question which those who complain about the wickets being too easy nowadays should have to answer is : "What is the cause of the almost weekly list of accidents and retired hurts which occurred, to take only one season, in 1935 ?" Is it not only on rough, or fiery, wickets that batsmen *should* get hit ?

My belief is that the over-prepared wicket complaint is exaggerated, and that the so-called "natural" wicket, prepared apparently by some unknown process by using only a mowing-machine and a roller, is an impossibility if first-class cricket is to remain first class.

Prepare wickets by using only mower and roller, as is suggested year after year, and the death-knell of first-class cricket would be only a question of a very short time.

I fear that in giving my views on the preparation of wickets I have strayed somewhat from the subject of my memories of Test cricket, but the two things, wickets and Tests, are so interwoven, so much the one being part of the other, that I must be excused for not trying to separate them.

I have already written of my double-nineties in the Test at Lord's in 1921. My feelings can be better imagined perhaps than I can describe them when in my next Australian Test on the same ground five years later I got into the eighties, on quite a good wicket, and so once again saw the "century in a Test at Lord's" dangling before my eyes. Again, however, it was not to be, for I was l.b.w. b Ryder 87. Actually, I had already made my hundred in a Test at Lord's two years previously, but that was against the South African team of 1924. I cannot imagine what kind of a cricketer he can be who is not content with a century in any Test match, but, at the same time, a century against the Australians in a Test match, and that, too, at the headquarters of the game, comes first. It has a hall-mark entirely its own.

Nothing can diminish its prestige, or the value which all cricketers attach to it.

I can say that it is the one disappointment of my otherwise supremely happy cricket career that this signal honour was denied me. To have got so near as 95, 93 and 87 in *successive* innings at Lord's was just one of those galling experiences which teaches us cricketers to take the rough with the smooth, and to turn up smiling for the next bout. Which no cricketer worthy the name has ever refused to do.

# CHAPTER V

## THE HILL AND THE GRILL

BARRACKERS are born, not made. Thank goodness England never had the prescription.

Who started the fashion of introducing this bad habit to the cricket grounds of Australia I do not profess to know.

That something of the behaviour which "killed" the last M.C.C. tour in Australia happened in the very distant past is evident from the experiences there of our revered past Kent captain, Lord Harris. I seem to have read something about his lordship's return to the pavilion, after the crowd had broken on to the ground, "armed with a stump." Mr. Jardine's tour in 1932–33 seems to have been a tea-party by comparison !

While I do not find it in me to have anything but a very strong objection to the whole atmosphere of barracking in its Australian character, I am happy to say that I never really fell foul of the barrackers myself.

Except, perhaps, on one occasion when it had been just my luck to be placed in the outfield plumb in front of "the Hill" at Sydney. That was on my first tour in Australia so this was by way of being my baptism of a kind of thing such as one never experiences in England. Somebody hit a ball in my direction and, as happens even to Bradman, I did not field it, a four resulting. That was the spark in the barrel of powder. Up she went !

"Why were you let out of school, eh ?" "Hi, ground-man, rig up a net behind him," "Skipper ! Keep him out here, he'll win it for us," were a few of the taunts flung at me, as though nobody ever made a mistake on the cricket field, and, what annoyed me in my innocence even more, as though the howlers themselves could have done so much better. It went on unceasingly. I stood it as long as I could in silence until a regular foghorn of a voice boomed out in the twang peculiar to so many Australians : "What you oughter have is a good big 'sack.' "

Turning sharply round, I flung the retort : "If I'd a sack as big as your mouth I'd . . ." I forget the rest, but whatever it was, it was drowned in a regular storm of cheers.

I had discovered the secret ! Ignore the barrackers and they dislike the sight of you. Remain silent, treat them as though they do not exist, and nothing is too bad for you—that is to say, in the shape of words, for I have never known of a case of actual violence perpetrated against any of our professional cricketers. But give the barracker just a little of his own back and he's a different person. Perhaps he is not singular in liking to be taken notice of.

It was the silence of Mr. Jardine on the tour prior to 1932–33 which I am inclined to believe got their backs up against him. That silence, with the famous Oxford Harlequin cap as a guide post, made him a permanent target for their idea of humour. Which is certainly not ours, I rejoice to think, when they descend to abuse. Because then human speech can scarcely go lower than that which is employed by what is, I am sure, only the worst section of the Australian cricket public. To me it is amazing that anybody can find one word in defence of "the Hill" at Sydney and "the Grill" at Melbourne at their worst.

At their best they occasionally do hit upon an amusing, if sometimes too personal, utterance. On that same tour Mr. Douglas was on one occasion in one of his most pertinacious moods with the ball.

Owing to repairs going on at one of the telegraph boards it was not in use, and he happened to be bowling from the end where the board that was in action was at his back.

He was not getting wickets, and the score was increasing at the right pace to keep the barrackers full of pep. Over after over Mr. Douglas kept plugging away, after walking back to the start of his "run" rubbing the ball on his forearm.

At last it came : "Now then, Johnny, why don't you have a go at the other end—you'll then be able to have a look at your analysis !" Which is, I think, one of the most apt remarks in the not meagre history of barrackers' efforts. To the reader who has not been to matches in Australia I must explain that their telegraph boards show run by run the runs scored off each bowler.

Of a more personal kind was the comment of another barracker, which I am sure my friend "Patsy" Hendren will pardon me for mentioning here, even though it may be a chestnut for some of my readers. On one of our upcountry games "Patsy" had been monkeying about a bit near the boundary, and the crowd was in good humour in consequence. During a lull a shrill voice piped out : "Ah, Pat, you'd be perfect, if you'd only got a tail."

But that there is a more serious side to this public nuisance, the barracker, is perfectly obvious. Here are the facts of the case when Messrs. Rockley Wilson and P. G. H. Fender fell foul of him, only because they had written the truth. This happened on the tour of 1920–21, and it nearly resulted in personal assault. The origin was a glaringly bad decision by an umpire.

Parkin and Waddington were at the wicket. A straight hit by Parkin was touched by the bowler, the ball going on and breaking the wicket at Waddington's end. Waddington had not backed up and had not moved out of his crease. The umpire, no doubt thinking he was himself about to be hit by the ball, had turned his face right round. But on the cry, "How's that?" he at once gave Waddington out.

You would scarcely think that such an almost everyday incident would result, as this did, in one of the hosts threatening to strike one of his guests with a stick, but that is what resulted.

Both Messrs. Wilson and Fender cabled their true versions of what had taken place to England. These were promptly cabled back by the London correspondents of Australian papers to their papers in Sydney —as "news," mark you!

That re-cabling started the fire; so you see the Press *has* something to answer for sometimes! Next day "the Hill" said what it thought, and, in case we had not heard the first time, repeated it, and then a few times more for luck. Until, as Waddington said, he almost wished he had backed up too far!

We expected "the Hill" to let itself go a bit on this occasion but we certainly did not expect the exhibition of bad manners that ensued in the members' pavilion. Members stood up and cursed Mr. Wilson loudly. One, after threatening to hit him with his stick as he came in from batting, appeared about to do so when he received the shock of his life. This took the form of Harry Makepeace, who sprang from the balcony of our dressing room, almost landing on the man's back, and squaring up, acquainted the menacing one with the fact that if he wanted to fight anyone he could start on Harry.

So, you see, the rumour that Yorkshire and Lancashire are always at one another's throats is so much eyewash. Here was a Yorkshireman in a tight corner finding his best and promptest defender in a Lancashire lad, and he, too, about the smallest of our party.

Actually when Mr. Wilson got back to the pavilion

that day the members fairly rose at him, and the whole situation became so menacing that had it not been for the instant action of Messrs. Noble, Iredale and Clem Hill, who rushed to Mr. Wilson as he reached the gate, and fairly carried him up into the dressing room, I am sure he would have been badly manhandled.

Mr. Fender, who was next in to bat, must have wondered if another war had started. But he did the one thing necessary, the thing which has its instant appeal where a cricket public whether in or out of temper is present. He hit a four at once. Those who had come to blame stayed to cheer him, and there is no doubt in my mind that his crisp free innings did much to relieve the tension.

But it is not to be supposed that the Australian barrackers had done with Mr. Wilson, or that this hooliganism is confined to the "Hill," and the hotter "Grill."

I have never sat in "the Grill" to watch cricket, and as it is said they don't need a thermos flask there to keep their tea hot I'm glad I've missed that experience.

Soon after the incident I have described at Sydney we had to play at Geelong. There a bushranger was permitted to hustle Mr. Wilson out of the gate when he went in to bat, while the local policeman—who no doubt knew his Dead-eye Dick—treated it as a great joke and joined in the general offensive laughter.

A little later on Mr. Wilson had another experience of how Australia loved him for speaking the truth. During a breathlessly hot train journey we all removed our coats. A gust of wind sent Mr. Wilson's—it *would* be his !—flying out of the window. What more natural, since in his pockets were valuable private papers, than that Mr. Wilson should pull the cord and stop the train. The guard was livid about this—simply, we thought, because it was Mr. Wilson. Actually he came near to being arrested on arrival at our destination !

As I have already written, I have no idea who started the barracking nuisance in Australia. It is clearer, however, who has allowed it to attain its present proportions. This is due to the encouragement which barrackers have consistently received in the Press, and to the fact that Australian cricket authorities did not grasp the nettle—when they saw it sprouting and growing—at the start. A little barracking goes a very long way, and it is difficult to get an Australian to understand how objectionable to their visitors the practice really is, once it has begun to overstep the clearly defined limit of legitimate openly expressed criticism. No cricketer that I have ever met expects applause all the time. If a cricketer misses a catch his ears are disappointed if they do not instantly hear the long drawn out "O-o-oh" with which cricket's faithful followers spontaneously give vent to their surprise or disappointment, whichever it is, at seeing a quite normal everyday happening. But such surprise or disappointment needs no further expression.

Cricket is a well-bred game. There is no room in it for anything but good manners. Barracking at its best is more or less harmless, at its worst it is an absolute pestilence and a spoil-sport. It looks to me, judging by the noise, to be an American importation, wherein all that is objectionable in the loud-mouthed behaviour of the fans of baseball has been transplanted on to cricket's fair and peaceful fields.

I know that some Australians think that we Englishmen are a bit thin-skinned about barracking. But surely the peace and orderliness of our cricket crowds is preferable to the din and insults of a barracking uproar ?

I have felt obliged to write as I have against the whole barracking business because of my intense love for cricket, and my consequent objection to anything which I think is calculated to harm it. Barracking run mad brings out anything that may be bad in any character. I have cited the only instance where the barrackers and I almost got to loggerheads. For the rest, I was always magnificently treated in Australia, where, on each of my four visits I always had most enjoyable times, quite apart from the never-failing pleasure of taking part in "needle" matches.

We, in England, do not perhaps always appreciate to the full the part which cricket plays in the national life of Australians. It is, with them, as fervent a religion as is Soccer to a Clackmannan boy. When Australia gets a really good player it does not merely just like, or take a fancy to him, it literally idolizes him, almost worships him. Let anyone now dare to suggest in Australia that Jack Hobbs or John Tyldesley were better batsmen than is Don Bradman and he will hear such a chorus as his ears can barely stand. They adored Victor Trumper—who, indeed, would not, for here was a man among men, leaving apart his artistry with the bat?

Of the barrackers, I give them this to their credit, that they are fairly impartial, or have been so far. Whether in 1932–33 had Australia had Gregory and Macdonald and England no Larwood, cricket's history would have been written differently, who can say?

But, in such a case, the impartiality of which I have just written would certainly have been tested!

An always present possibility, and consequent cause of friction, is the extraordinary amount of notice which the Australian Press take of the barrackers. Perhaps this is done on the principle of "don't ignore him and he's all right," of which I have just written. But when taking notice of him, such comment as is made should be, at any rate, accurate. I am thinking as I write this about what happened on the 1920–21 tour in Australia in the fifth Test. Jack Hobbs was limping a bit, a strained thigh muscle I believe was the cause. One of the Australians hit a four past cover, and it so happened that it was Jack's job to fetch the ball from the boundary. Some of the barrackers, however, thought that one of the other fielders—like extra-cover, for example—might have saved Jack the trouble, so they started chipping, not Jack, but his colleagues. This little matter was magnified in the Press into a kind of general accusation of unfair barracking of Hobbs.

Though I was not there on the 1932–33 tour, I suspect that a great many things were published in the Australian papers which, because the only result of reading them would be to inflame the more rowdy elements in the crowd, would have been much better left unwritten.

We, for our part, should also do well to consider the effect upon barrackers of the visit of an English team. For them it has some, at least, of the air of an "outing," of a sort of festival. Our cricket public gets cricket for six days a week over a period of four months or more annually.

In Australia the four headquarters grounds—Adelaide, Melbourne, Sydney and Brisbane—only see three Sheffield Shield matches each per season. So that the appearance of an English eleven in itself, quite apart from any such possibly provocative factor as Larwood's style of bowling or the unpopularity, imagined or otherwise, of any member of the visiting team, provides such an outlet for pent-up feelings that we over here can scarcely understand. After all, when a large mass of humanity is more or less on holiday indulging, shall we put it at its worst, in a sort of "beano," it is comprehensible that a very tiny spark might start a very large conflagration. That is why all comment at the time should go out of its way to be as calm and accurate as possible For the good of Australian cricket it is to be hoped the last has been heard of *offensive* barracking. For it is probable that should our next team out there have to suffer this infliction not only will it be, after that, difficult to persuade our amateurs to make the journey, but professionals also will think twice before accepting the invitation.

Our cricketers can now get their fill of other tours abroad under thoroughly pleasant conditions.

# CHAPTER VI

## "THAT FRIEND THOU HAST . . ."

It having been suggested to me that some of the most famous of cricketers, with and against whom I have played, might like to contribute to this book, I have been very fortunate indeed in receiving the following kind replies to my request. These are from captains of England and of Kent, of Australia and of South Africa.

I shall always very greatly treasure the many nice things they have been so kind as to write.

From Lord Hawke (President and ex-Captain 27 years of Yorkshire County C.C. ; President of M.C.C., 1914–18 ; present Treasurer of M.C.C.).

"Dear Woolley,

"Being a Northerner and a Tyke, and having had many hard battles with you on the field, I think it is very nice of you to ask me to send a short contribution to the book of your reminiscences, which I am delighted to hear is shortly to be published.

"You and I have known each other on the field of play more years than I care to count. My admiration for you as a cricketer and a man commenced from the earliest days, and I am sure has increased each year.

"If I compare you to Georgie Hirst in greatness as a cricketer I think you will be proud to be so connected.

"As a man I have always known you as a Sahib, and my only regret is that, in producing your book now, you have missed all that my great friend, Lord Harris, would have said of you. I, for one who am not a Kent man, know how much he held you in the highest esteem, and regarded you as a worthy example of all that is best in our national game.

"May I mention two of your great innings, of which it was my good fortune to see every ball ? You scored over ninety in each innings in the Australian Test at Lord's in 1921.

"If you had never played any other innings than those two your name would be handed down for all time in the highest class of cricket. I shall always remember how on those days you put the bat against the ball when England was in dire distress. You could not save her, but that was not your fault.

"In my opinion, your greatest service to English cricket, and with it to the game wherever it is played, has been that throughout your brilliant career you have been the most consistent exponent of the idea that the ball is there to be hit, and not patted, or played with the pads. Your strokes through the covers, and sometimes brilliant cuts, were a joy in my day, and ever since I have continued to revel in them.

"Your idea of the game is the true one. If all players followed your example there would no longer be the cry of poor gates.

"I wish you luck, and sincerely hope that your book reaps the reward which your brilliant playing career and popular personality so richly deserve."

HAWKE.

Xmas, 1935.

From MR. J. R. MASON (Captain of Kent ; England in Australia, 1898).

"My Dear Frank,

"I well remember hearing about the promise you were showing at the "Nursery" at Tonbridge in 1903, in which year you were engaged to take part in the morning practice and play in a match or two if required, but before the year 1903 you, then living at Tonbridge, were frequently to be found on the Tonbridge cricket ground, where your natural ability both as batsman and bowler was recognized by the Kent authorities even then. In the two following years, 1904 and 1905, you did well in Club and ground and various other matches, and in 1906 you played for the County.

"I was not playing in your first match at Old Trafford against Lancashire, but I know your start was not a great one, as on the first day you failed to score, missed two catches and took only one wicket for a hundred and three runs ; however, on the last morning of the match you played a great innings of sixty-four, but better things were in store. I saw you play in your third County match against Surrey at the Oval, when you did extraordinarily well, taking three Surrey wickets, clean bowling Hayward, Hayes and Goatly, quite a nice bag. You proceeded to play a splendid innings of seventy-two and in Surrey's second innings you obtained five wickets for eighty runs. In the last innings you made twenty-three not out at a very critical stage of the match, as when Arthur Fielder, No. 11 batsman, came in nineteen runs were wanted to win the match, Kent winning by one wicket. This all-round performance established your reputation and since then you have gone from strength to strength.

"I cannot recapitulate your many fine performances both for Kent and England, but I must mention certain matches in which you made cricket history  Against Middlesex at Lord's in 1908 Kent declared their second innings at 4 o'clock on the last day, leaving Middlesex two hundred and five to win and rather less than two hours to bat. We did not seem to have a chance of getting them out in that time and a draw appeared inevitable, but you went on to bowl at the Pavilion end and in four overs and three balls dismissed six batsmen for eight runs and we won with ten minutes to spare—a fine performance.

"Another match I distinctly remember was at Stourbridge in 1909 against Worcester, when Fielder and you put on two hundred and thirty-five runs for the last wicket, a record which stood for some time, but has now been beaten.

"In that same year 1909 you became a cricketer by bagging 0 and 0 against Lancashire at Tonbridge.

"I have not been able since the War to see you play in many matches but I was fortunate enough to see you play in 1921 at Lord s against Australia, getting ninety-five and ninety-three when things were going very badly for England and with Macdonald and Gregory bowling against you in their best form.

"I believe you have visited both Australia and South Africa four times and made many big scores in both countries.

"I hope, Frank you will be able to play for several more seasons, as a young cricketer can learn a great deal from watching you at the wicket and in the field."

Yours sincerely,<br>J. R. MASON.

From MR. H. D. G. LEVESON-GOWER (President of Surrey County C.C , Captain of Surrey, and of England in South Africa).

"Frank Woolley is versatile.

' A great—very great—left-hand batsman. A few years back a great left-hand bowler. Has kept wicket for England in a Test match.

"Has played golf—but not yet for England—and now, in his own words, he is playing his first literary innings. Many compliments.

"Naturally, I can pay to this 'new author' compliments deserved, but he has done me an honour in asking me to write a letter to be included in a chapter to which cricketers are contributing. I appreciate to the full this honour, for it gives me an opportunity of expressing my admiration of his skill as a cricketer, and my gratitude for the many pleasures I have derived from playing with him and against him, and as an onlooker.

"I must confess, however, that practically the first time I saw him I was not so pleased with him. I think I am right in saying that it was in 1906 that Woolley first came into the Kent side. At any rate, I have a very vivid recollection of a magnificent performance of his at the Oval that year. Surrey and Kent is a miniature Test match, and in that match, with about 20 runs to win, and the last man in (Fielder), Surrey's hopes of a victory ran high. But she reckoned without 'Young Woolley,' who rose to the occasion and, taking charge of the bowling himself with the confidence of a veteran, enabled Kent to get home after a thrilling finish.

"His share in the match, 3 wickets for 37 in the first innings, 5 wickets for 82 in the second ; 72 runs in the first, 23 not out in the second innings.

"I have mentioned this match to show that from a very successful debut in first-class cricket he has never looked back. No—Woolley did not give me pleasure in that match !

"In the winter of 1909-10 I captained the M.C.C. team in South Africa. I was fortunate enough to have Woolley with me—I fancy it was the first time he had ever been on tour. He was, of course, a great asset, but he never quite did himself justice. He was frequently given out l.b.w.—so much so, that it was a joke amongst us all.

" 'Bent your knee again, Frank,' we used to say ; though I must own that on one occasion he was nearly at short leg in playing at a ball to avoid another l.b.w. decision—when the umpire's finger went up— and pointed the way to the Pavilion for Woolley's edification !

"I was going in next and commiserated with him on the decision.  His reply was : 'Keep as far away from the wicket, captain, as you can, or you will join me pretty soon.'

"His words were prophetic—I was with him in a few minutes.

"Have you ever heard Woolley really laugh ?  I have ! He laughed for a fortnight in South Africa after an incident that happened at a dinner we attended during the tour.  And when we meet now we recall that evening and his laughter is renewed.

In fact, if I remember rightly, it was the recollection of that dinner in South Africa that caused him to miss a putt when I was one of his opponents in a foursome at Sundridge Park, in the annual golf match that Mr. B. A. Glanvill very kindly arranges, Kent v. Surrey cricketers.

"The incident referred to was that the proposer of the toast of the M.C.C. inadvertently substituted another letter (lower down in the alphabet) for the first two.

"Where does one place Woolley amongst the famous left-handed batsmen is a question I have heard frequently asked.  In my mind, he is one of the finest I have ever seen.  I am not forgetting Clem Hill, Bardsley, Francis Ford or Percy Chapman, to mention only a few.

"There is no batsman in England even to-day whose style is more commanding to watch.  There are few whose driving and perfect timing can give the spectator, be he expert or not, more genuine pleasure.

"In conclusion, imagine, if you will, one who loves the 'game,' who has done much for his County and for Test cricket, and there you have Frank Woolley, whom cricketers delight to play with and against, and whom spectators delight to honour."

H. D. G. LEVESON GOWER.

A BIT OF FOOT-WORK AT HOME!
A push-stroke off the left with a long-handled grip

## CORRECT FOOTWORK

A four to leg off Allen by Ponsford at the Oval, August, 1934
The position of Ponsford's right foot shows how full is the use that a great player makes
of the ground between the bowling and the popping creases

From MR. P. F. WARNER (Captain of England and
   Middlesex).

"During the Canterbury Week, some years ago,
Woolley had just got out after playing one of his most
beautiful innings, and I recollect G. L. V. Weigall
careering across the ground at the end of the day and
saying, so that all might hear : 'Don't talk to me, sir,
of your Trumpers and your Ranjis. This Woolley is
the very best any of us have ever seen, or ever will
see."

"Mr. Weigall is a sound judge of cricket, even if, on
occasions, excess of zeal coupled with an intense
enthusiasm and local pride leads him on ; and while
my own view is that comparisons between the really
great cricketers are extremely difficult to make, there
are many, including myself, who would rather see
Woolley bat than anyone else.

"For sheer grace he has never been surpassed, if
indeed equalled.

"I have seen Woolley play so often, and so splendidly,
that it is not easy to pick out any particular incident
or innings, but there are three moments in his career
that stick in my memory. All of them, curiously
enough, within a few months of each other.

"The first was at Melbourne, in 1912, in a Test
match, when he drove R. B. Minnett straight for six
into the grand stand. At first the ball seemed to be
going into the hands of the deep field—W. Bardsley,
I think—who actually put up his hands to make the
catch, but it rose gradually as it gained speed, and
eventually passed some twelve or fifteen feet over the
deep fieldsman's head, and hit the stand with that
lovely sound—to a cricketer—leather meeting wood.
Never have I seen a ball travel so fast with so little
apparent effort on the part of the batsman. Woolley
seemed merely to stroke the ball.

"The second was at Sydney, about three weeks later, and this time it was a catch, at second slip, that Woolley made off the bowling of S. F. Barnes. One ball went fast and low to the left of Woolley, who made an acrobatic dive at it and held it with his left hand while appearing to turn a somersault.

"The very best slip catch I have ever seen was by Woolley's captain, A. P. F. Chapman, off Tate at the Oval, in 1928, in the Test match v. the West Indies.

"I bracket Woolley's catch with R. E. Foster's at Sydney, in the Test match in December 1903, which dismissed V. Trumper, c. Foster b. Arnold !

"The third was at Lord's, on May 27th, 1912, when an M.C.C. Australian team met the Rest of England. Woolley was batting to that fine fast bowler, Walter Brearley, who was on at the Nursery end. Mr. Brearley sent down a ball which was only just short of a length and Woolley flung his bat 'lazily' at it. The next second the ball was scattering the spectators at the top of the Mound stand. It was an amazing stroke. I had a near view of it for I was in at the other end.

"I am no judge of cards, but my wife, I understand, has some reputation in this respect, and she tells me that Woolley was a very good bridge player. At all events, whenever they drew together as partners on the voyage to Australia in 1911 onlookers used to declare that it was—'murder !'

"For the rest, Woolley is one of the easiest people to like I have ever met. His gentle voice and quiet manner appeal to me, and on a tour there could be no more loyal, pleasant and helpful companion. I have never known him to be anything else but very nice.

"That his name will go down to posterity as one of the greatest cricketers the game has ever produced is as certain as to-morrow morning's sun. It was I who wrote of him as 'The Pride of Kent,' and I am proud of it, for it is true."

P. F. WARNER.

From M. A. NOBLE (ex-Captain of Australia).

"To correctly assess the real capacity of a cricketer and ascertain his greatness under all conditions one must have had personal contact with him on the field of play. There is no other reliable test than an extensive opportunity of bowling or batting against him. Then one gains an intimate knowledge of those attributes familiar to the expert and necessary for the equipment of a champion, which for ever remain unrevealed to those who are merely onlookers, however well-equipped they may be, or however clever their judgment.

"I regret that Frank Woolley and I never met on the Test cricket field. (However, I have read, nodded. Noble captained Australia at the Oval in my first Test.—F. E. W.)

"Therefore, this account of perhaps one of the best fighting and most brilliant Test knocks I ever saw must, of necessity, be given from the point of view of careful observation over the fence.

"The first Test match of the 1924–25 series on the Sydney Cricket Ground ran into the seventh day. It was a succession of big scores, surprises, collapses and recoveries. The two greatest recoveries occurring in the second innings of each side, both being the result of unsuspected courage and ability of two tail-enders in association with the most brilliant batsmen of their respective teams. Australia made 450 and England replied with 298. In the second innings Australia had lost 9 for 355 when Mailey joined Taylor. This partnership added 127 runs, taking the score to 452, thus breaking the previous Australian Test record for the tenth wicket, held by Duff and Armstrong, 120 runs in 1901–02.

"England had to face the colossal task of getting 615 runs to win. Nothing daunted, they fought every inch of the journey. Though they did not attain their goal, their fight for runs was characterized by British determination, courage and resource, with a climax as entertaining and inspiring as any previous struggle in the long succession of Test matches, which had converted what threatened to be overwhelming loss into glorious defeat.

"With 8 down for 276 the match appeared to be all over when Freeman joined Woolley. Then the miracle happened.

"These two Kent players, worthy sons of the garden of England, neither of whom had scored in the first innings, defied the attack of the Australian bowlers in a manner that will remain an everlasting illustration of the old adage that a match is never lost until it is won. Woolley made 123, the top score of the match, and Freeman 50 not out. They put on 128 runs for the ninth wicket, the final score being 411.

"Woolley obviously suffered from a bad knee during the whole of his innings, and this was, I think, the cause of his eventual dismissal. He pasted fast, medium pace and slow bowlers with tremendous power. His well-known forceful, straight and cover drives were made with that swinging pendulum-like bat which connected unerringly with the ball and sent it to the boundary with the pace of a pistol shot. A forward and outward movement of the right foot, and a swiftly moving bat, in complete harmony with his mental urge, sent a square drive whizzing past cover point, who, unable to move in time to intercept it, stood astonished at its speed. Again, a short rising ball was square or late cut quick as thought ; here a pull to long on, there a cunningly executed leg glance, all making glorious continuity in an innings sparkling with skill, artistry and power.

"Thousands of runs are appreciated under favourable conditions, but those made in adversity, when it is a case of do or die, remain in the mind while memory lasts.

"By that innings Woolley carved for himself a niche in the temple of the immortals, where none but the names of the courageous aristocracy of our national game may be inscribed."

M. A. Noble.

From H. W. Taylor (Captain of South Africa).

"Frank Woolley will always be remembered by South African cricketers who played against him in England as the 'bogey man.' This great respect for his batting ability is, I know, shared by the Australians. Although, perhaps, Frank was not so successful against them as he has been against us during the post-War period, I know they always gave a sigh of relief when they got him out for a small total.

"In 1924 he completely mastered our bowlers with his graceful polished strokes ; always out to punish the bowling, and *playing everything sideways, as the game should be played* ; perfect footwork in his forward and back play which made all bowling look easy.

"In Woolley, England had a master batsman whom everybody should have striven to emulate, yet Hammond is the only English player in recent years who appears to play on similar lines.

"Reverting back to 1924. Frank had been punishing our bowling unmercifully in the matches he had played against us, and when it came to the Kent match, Blanckenberg said the only thing to do to the 'bogey man' was to bowl wide off-theory.

"We tried it ; but the wider our fellows bowled the harder he hit the ball. In the end we had five fellows on the off boundary, yet they couldn't stop the fours. The 170 odd he made was a masterpiece.

"When we started the Tests against England in 1929, Frank was left out of the first two Tests and we rubbed our hands with glee. We knew we had a chance against England without him.

"We used to read the county matches and we could see he was beginning to strike form. Our spirits drooped a little as we knew he was pushing himself into the England XI. In the third Test he arrived and changed the whole complexion of the game. His two fine knocks gave England the victory.

"At Manchester he dominated the game with a magnificent century.

"He is the greatest left-handed batsman I have played against, and if England can find another as good they will indeed be fortunate."

HERBY TAYLOR.

"Johannesburg,
    "Nov. 22nd, 1935."

# CHAPTER VII

## SOME THUMBNAIL SKETCHES

BEGINNING with Victor Trumper and ending with S. F. Barnes, I have tried in this chapter to sketch briefly some of the characteristics of a few Test cricketers.

I decided to write about two teams of them. But which 22 ? That was the question.

So I put fifty picked names in a hat, and drew out twenty-two. The luck of the draw gave me Victor Trumper as No. 1. I did not dispute that ! When, however, the twenty-second name appeared and Barnes was not among them I could not assuage my disappointment by any other means than by including him on the strength of luck in odd numbers.

Twenty-two cricketers and Barnes not among them ! Could anything be more absurd ?

But the luck of the draw has given me two teams without a wicket-keeper between them ! Well, perhaps that has happened in real life, so I will carry on.


### THE LATE VICTOR TRUMPER.

I have written about Trumper more than once in this book. He was one in a thousand, whether on or off "the middle." A grand character.

There is a story which they never tire of telling about Victor, which proves what a splendid chap he was. It concerns a match in New Zealand. Just as Victor was walking in to bat with "Horseshoe" Collins a small boy ran out to him and said, "I wish, Mr. Trumper, you would use my bat," and offered him a youth's sized bat.

"All right, sonny, I'll try," and he handed his own bat to the boy with a, "You hang on to this till I come out, I won't be long."

"Why, Victor, you're surely not going to use that thing?" said Collins as they walked on.

"I simply couldn't refuse the kiddie," was all Victor said. He kept the owner waiting a fair time, but at last the bat split from end to end.

It is understood that it holds an honoured place, repaired and bound, in a New Zealand home. And no wonder.

Trumper was a natural batsman, who revealed his greatness by the time he seemed to have to spare for each stroke, and the different scoring strokes he seemed to have for what looked to the bowler, and the field, to be the same ball.

Nobody I ever saw, and here I include K. S. Ranjitsinhji, could cut a straight ball with Trumper's accuracy. Strict coaches would fault him for attempting that stroke, and I should certainly do all in my power if I was coaching a youngster to put a stop to any such attempts.

Such strokes are only for Trumpers, not for the rest of us.

A very smart and accurate field, Victor, who could throw over 100 yards, had a beautiful low trajectory return.

Such men as he was adorn our game in all they do, their name and fame are imperishable.

## The late Mr. K. L. Hutchings.

I never see a "silly" point positioned on a hard wicket without wishing Mr. Hutchings—the hardest driver I ever saw, bar nobody—was at the wicket, or was in next.

Mr. Hutchings was the only batsman who did, or

probably could, make George Hirst retreat at mid-off. Very strongly built about the loins and shoulders and extremely lissom at the wrists, when Mr. Hutchings got hold of an off-drive then there is no doubt the ball exceeded the limit. It became as near the shot-out-of-a-gun, of which we read and hear so much, and often quite undeservedly, as a ball hit by a bat could ever approach in speed. If he had not got himself out so often this very attractive player would have made the cricket world ring with his name. He was the best puncher we had in Kent in my time.

A grand outfield, he had an extraordinarily fast return considering that he threw the ball with a characteristic below the shoulder wristy delivery that I have never seen in any other player.


E. HENDREN.

The best fellow in the world to field alongside in the slips when 400 is on the board, only one wicket down, a cloudless sky, and a scratchless pitch.

A grand little cricketer, and what a fellow traveller. No voyage is dull or train journey tedious when Patsy's aboard.

He's always up to something, and succeeds in never overdoing it.

The only thing I've ever seen him overdo is tenure of the wicket against Kent!

Even so, I'd rather Patsy got runs than many others, as he could not play dull if he tried.

Patsy took a little time in arriving, but there was no doubt about it once he had come. I am not perhaps so good at other people's figures as I ought to be, but I should be surprised if any other county cricketer has accomplished on his home ground such a record as Patsy has made at Lord's. It must be unique. For years no visiting eleven began to breathe freely there until Hendren's second innings was ended.

Hendren's batting has all the strokes, if I except the genuine cut, which is not the same thing as saying that he cannot cut. Like all stubby men—George Hirst was one—Patsy can hook as well as anyone. Some of his hooks have become almost legendary. They have been more expensive to the opposition than most hooks because most people are content with fours. But Patsy plays the same stroke hitting the ball slightly underneath, so it goes over instead of only to the boundary.

Patsy has been one of the few great players who make frequent and correct use of his fore-foot.

You have all read about Patsy's crooked bat. All I can say is, that it has got a good big straight bit as well, and that that straight bit has an uncanny knack of connecting with the ball at the right time. If Patsy really has a crooked bat, then what would have been the dimensions of that record at Lord's had it been straight ? Or are we all a bit fanatical about the crime of a crooked bat ? Sometimes I wonder.

A splendid fielder anywhere, most of Patsy's bowling has been done either before the game began or after a wicket has fallen, when, with characteristic impudence, he shows his mates how they might have got rid of the departed batsman much more cheaply. Still, he has bowled in a Test match.

Long ago he played himself into the hearts of the cricket-loving public, and I know I announce no news when I say that no cricketer ever did more than he to keep alive public interest in cricket. He is a living embodiment of the joy in cricket when it is properly played, lightheartedly but seriously.


MAURICE TATE.

One of the greatest bowlers of my time—a genuine world-beater in his best day.

His bowling had the priceless assets of length, of life, and of what seemed to be a surprisingly great increase of pace after pitching without that extra speed being revealed by his action.

The true type of hostile bowler, always attacking, and giving the batsman no rest.

This hostility was his greatest asset to the National Eleven. All the greatest Australian bowlers have it. Not enough of ours have it. Barnes, Mr. F. R. Foster, George Hirst, Tate, Macaulay and Mr. G. O. Allen are the best we have had in my time.

Tate's best ball to me was the one that pitched on or about my leg-stump, and which, unless played, hit the middle and off-stump. To right-handed batsmen that is the one which hits their leg-stump, or which brings about an l.b.w. decision. Though even in his best day Maurice was not a true off-break bowler, there is no doubt that by body action, and the natural angle, he could make the ball go away from a left-handed batsman, or, apparently, come back to hit a right-hander's leg stump. But this was done off the pitch, not through the air.

I have never seen Tate spin a ball either way.

Whether or not it is possible for a bowled cricket ball to *increase* its pace after striking the pitch is a matter which I do not propose to attempt to discuss here. Some cricketers think this is possible, others hold the contrary opinion. But I feel sure that Tate often bowls a ball which very successfully conveys to the batsman, and probably to the wicket-keeper also, the impression that that ball was not so fast through the air as it was off the pitch. Perhaps an attempt will be made ere long to prove or disprove whether fast bowlers can make a ball go faster off the pitch than it was through the air. At present any opinion either way seems pure conjecture. I would like to see this matter scientifically proved or disproved. But it is by no means clear how a cricket ball can add to its

pace after striking the ground, at which moment, as
is obvious, its pace through the air was decreasing.

Maurice Tate, when he was sent in first for Sussex
by Mr. Arthur Gilligan, was often a very awkward
customer for the opponents of Sussex because he held
straight and gave the ball lots of those broad loins
and grand forearms. His batting was as pugnacious
as his bowling.

One of the cheeriest of triers, Maurice is a great
chap to have on your side on or off the field, for it
does not matter a bit what the score-board looks like
that smile never wears off and that chin never droops.

He is the sort that makes cricket a happy game.
No team but is all the better if Maurice is playing for
it. A Sussex ground without Maurice and his pipe is
an aspect not to be considered with any comfort.

Happily, as he is only 41, and the supply of pipes,
so long as Mr. Baldwin is Prime Minister, will be
unlimited, that sad day is far distant.

## THE LATE J. T. TYLDESLEY.

It was my good fortune to field while "Johnny"
made the highest score of his brilliant career. I have
explained elsewhere how he did not carry his figures
on that occasion into the fourth hundred. A pure
accident prevented him.

"Johnny" was a great batsman all round the wicket,
with the square cut and a purposeful hit over mid-off
as probably his greatest strokes.

He goes down to cricket with Arthur Shrewsbury,
so I am told, and Victor Trumper, and Jack Hobbs
as one of the four greatest batsmen, not counting
Grace, on a really difficult wicket.

I understand that Johnny was rarely, if ever,
stumped. Here is the secret. When he lunged out
forward he never overreached and dragged his foot.

I give the reason for this. Having lunged out and missed the ball, he avoided dragging or lifting his right toe by the simple process of letting his right leg pivot round (turning towards the off) on his hip, so that all the time the right toe remained touching the ground. At the end of the stroke the top of the toe was on the ground—the despair of the wicket-keeper, who had either already broken the wicket, having made sure the toe must lift (bad wicket-keeping that), or was there at the bails ball in hand, waiting like a cat watching a mouse for the one movement necessary for the sealing of a fate. Thus Johnny, who was the despair of bowlers, was a source of exasperation for wicket-keepers also.

He was a grand third-man and out. He is included in the ranks of the Immortals of Cricket because he was a member of that great England eleven at Birmingham in May, 1902—in which game he made 138 with a borrowed bat—which got Australia out for 36 (Rhodes 7 for 17, and Hirst 3 for 15). As some regard that as the strongest eleven that was ever seen on the same field, I give its names in their batting order : Mr. A. C. MacLaren (capt.), Mr. C. B. Fry, K. S. Ranjitsinhji, Mr. F. S. Jackson, J. T. Tyldesley, A. A. Lilley, G. H. Hirst, Mr. G. L. Jessop, L. C. Braund, W. H. Lockwood, and W. Rhodes. England made 376 for 9, Australia 36 and 46 for 2.

## KUMAR SHRI DULEEPSINHJI.

I have seen some of the Kumar Shri's most brilliant innings because of his quick-footed treatment of "Tich" Freeman, off whom he made more runs when "Tich" was at his best than any other player.

To "Duleep," as we all know and love him, belongs, I believe, the record of being the only county cricketer to make 300 runs in an innings on the same day, which he did in 1930 against Northants. Though one can never tell at this game, he is likely to be the holder of that record, if indeed it is his, in perpetuity. Unless Bradman or Hammond relieves him of it. Nobody else bats in the right way to beat such a marvellous performance. Previously "Duleep's" uncle, then K. S. Ranjitsinhji, with two separate centuries on the same day for Sussex v. Yorkshire, had achieved an even more difficult feat, so that between them this justly celebrated pair gave the rest of us something to be going on with.

A very strong part in "Duleep's" game was his placing power. He made such a big proportion of his runs in fours. Probably more in that way than anyone except Bradman.

He was the best cutter in the game in my time, without exception.

A brilliant slip fielder, he could not have been anything but a good one in any position.

His ill-health caused a very serious and, needless to add, a very much regretted loss to the game. Such artists with the bat are rarely seen, and when to such finished ability is joined a cheery, plucky temperament, the sadder the loss, both to him and his countless admirers.

## MAURICE LEYLAND.

A batsman after my own heart. No fours go a-begging once Leyland has got anything like a sight of the ball. The ball is there, the bat is in his hand—thud !

Maurice is not so deft off his legs as, for instance, Phil Mead, but that is because hit rather than deflection or push is his trump. Maurice has one of the soundest strokes past mid-on in the whole game, and he hits that cover drive a rare crack also.

So often does he succeed when a brace of wickets have not totted up the runs expected of them that his motto must be "The greater the difficulty the better the fun."

He has put on too much solid weight to be any longer in the top flight as an outfield, but earlier on he was very good indeed in the deep.

A very popular typical Tyke, Leyland, at 36, should be most useful to the National side for many more years to come.

## H. W. TAYLOR.

Here was a great attacking batsman, stronger perhaps on hard than soft wickets, but a genuine bat-against-ball player, of true Test quality.

He proved that against Barnes, who I never saw better played than the South African captain played him. Taylor, though essentially an off-side player, was very strong and accurate with the hook. He was always a dashing field who "made" the few yards towards an advancing ball as quickly as anyone I know.

A most popular man and charming opponent, he ranks very high indeed among South African born cricketers.

## C. G. MACARTNEY.

Was one of the very greatest of all Australian cricketers. Not so complete a batsman as Victor Trumper, because he had not Victor's cutting ability, but one of those batsmen who was attractive even when not scoring. Which was a rare sight, because bowlers who could keep Charlie quiet were not numerous.

A distinctly hostile batsman who always looked as

if he was going to make runs.   Very strong past mid-on,
Charlie was no dullard on the off-side.

I don't know how Australian bowlers attacked him,
but ours went too much for his leg stump.   Nowhere
more so than during that magnificent hundred before
lunch at Leeds in 1926.

He is the only batsman who has made a hundred
before lunch in a Test match who has also won a Test
with his bowling.   At Leeds in 1909 Macartney's
figures were :—

| O | M | R | W |
|------|---|----|---|
| 25.3 | 6 | 58 | 7 |
| 16.5 | 5 | 27 | 4 |

and he took the wickets of Johnny Tyldesley, Mr. A. C.
MacLaren and Sid Barnes twice each, and of Hobbs,
Sharp, Rhodes, Hirst, and Mr. Brearley ;  six clean
bowled, Mr. MacLaren, Hobbs and Hirst among
them.

He retired from big cricket at least ten years too
soon.   He always held that three days are enough for
any match—and he was quite right.

His 345 at Trent Bridge in 1921 against Notts, the
greatest hitting innings ever played there, proved his
theory to be correct.


J. B. Hobbs.

My regret, when I approach the subject of Jack
Hobbs, is that others seem to have used up all the
words in the English language on the same topic.
Repetition is no crime, and, to be sure, cricketers are
accustomed to it, so, since one cannot really have too
much of a good thing, I continue.

Hobbs made the mistake of not being born in Kent,
but he certainly did much to atone for this at Black-

heath, where he used to stay so long at the wicket that he appeared sometimes to be trying to qualify by residence for my county.

Not that he was unsuccessful against us at the Oval, but I cannot say why a batsman who plays a long innings against us at Blackheath always runs the risk of becoming unpopular with Kentish folk ! Our genial old foe, Tom Hayward, was another who used to take that risk on the same wicket, pushing his chocolate cap further and further back as the day wore on. That we always regarded as a most ominous sign, the gloom of which only the ever-pert optimism of "Charlie" Blythe could relieve. "Charlie" always said he'd got both Tom and Jack in his bag. Personally, I think it was round about fifty-fifty in this triangular duel. Anyway, Jack carried on Tom's Blackheath tradition of generally being what the Americans call jay-walkers, a "nuisance on foot," at the Rectory Field.

As regards Jack's cricket, I feel I am going to run counter to popular opinion in what I have to say about it.

There were two Jacks, the Pre- and the Post-War Jack. The *real* one was the Pre-War. Those of my readers who have seen only the Post-War one, especially after he had had a severe operation, in addition to thigh-muscle injury, have little idea of what the genuine article was like. Some batsman !

On sticky wickets or against good googlie bowling, only John Tyldesley and Charlie Macartney equalled, I do not say, excelled, Jack.

I did not see enough of the late Jam Sahib of Nawanagar in his prime to mention him here, and as I never saw Dr. Grace bat I cannot, of course, write of him.

In a different way both K. S. Duleepsinhji and the Nawab of Pataudi come within the bounds of my present considerations, but I did not see enough of either of these two when the ball was "talking" to be in a position to compare them with Hobbs. Moreover,

E

neither of them have had to cope with Pre-War bowling.

Most of Jack's hundreds and big feats were accomplished after the War, but I feel confident that he himself knows that his best cricket achievements were ante-1915.

To my way of looking on the matter, Jack's fielding in the last ten years of his career was even more wonderful than his batting. I question if ever before anyone has retained quickness of foot and hand movement, not to mention that of eye, so late in life to the amazing extent Jack did. When well over the forty mark he was even more agile than many young men under 25. The accuracy of his grasp of the ball at cover and the pace of its return to the wicket-keeper—how very rarely he threw to the bowler's end !—were simply astonishing long after he had passed the age at which cricketers are apt to complain that the ground seems much further away than it was.

I shall never forget one throw of Jack's, this time to the bowler's end. It was in the 1912 Australian Test at the Oval. Bardsley, batting to that very fine Lancashire left-hander, Dean, played a ball square rather gently. Jack was at cover point and there was no point. When he fielded the ball he was practically square with the batman's wicket and running towards gully. But he found time to hit the wicket at Dean's end, Bardsley being given run out ; a magnificent bit of fielding, perfect from start to finish.

A quieter, more modest chap than Jack Hobbs can seldom have played a big part in the cricket of the world. If he had been a conceited fellow, well, he would have had some justification ! But his long-sustained success never spoiled Jack. He soon established himself popular with his brother professionals, and he remained so to his retirement. He surely never made an enemy.

One strong dislike he had—the sea. I don't know

how many times he visited Australia and South Africa, but I'm sure he would have done so more often if he could have travelled overland.

## PHILIP MEAD.

We know what they say about old soldiers ; also about brooks. Well, Philip is in one of those out-fits.

Surely there never was another batsman so polite to the bowler as is my old friend Philip ? As one of them said to me : "I feel I ought to bow to him before I deliver each ball." You see, Philip touches his cap six times an over—or, more accurately, before each ball bowled to him. He also shuffles up with three movements to get into his final stance.

So now the industrious reader can start sums and find out how many times Philip has touched his cap while scoring over 50,000 runs, and how many yards he has shuffled before getting down to it.

He and Jack Hobbs began first-class cricket the same year, 1905. It has been announced that his aggregate and that of Hobbs in first-class cricket *in England* was identical when Jack retired. I am glad the responsibility of proving the truth of that announcement does not rest with me, as I know one acknowledged statistician who disagrees with it.

When Mead left the Oval to qualify for Hampshire he was a useful left-handed slow bowler whose batting ability not even he himself suspected. That developed later, until he became Trumper's equal at making runs off the good length ball, though in a different way.

The certainty of his placing strokes on either side of short-leg was his greatest asset in his best day.

If the field captain was compelled to pack the leg-side to stop the fours the process left a hole somewhere on the off-side through which Philip's strong forearm push, rather than drive, sent the ball with a frequency that was the despair of bowlers and captains.

I have never forgotten the way in which he out-manœuvred Warwick Armstrong at the Oval in 1921, when he made England's individual Test record in England of 182 not out.   Gregory, Macdonald, Mailey, and Armstrong bowled 127 overs between them in that innings, so they all had a try at him without success.

On the same ground Philip got, I am told, a good hundred last season against Surrey, the runs accumulating down the same non-stop roads.   But for his severe illness some years ago, when he had a very narrow shave, Mead would have been much higher in the centuries and aggregate list than he is.

As he is still only a kid of 49, there are many more hundreds to come.   Which will be good news for the many bowlers who need to learn their job.


## W. R. HAMMOND.

Wally is one of the rare kind of cricketer who arrives about once in every twenty years or so, like, in the past, Trumper, Hobbs, John Tyldesley and Macartney, born cricketers all of them, not made ones.

Without knowing it I should cheerfully risk the guess that in his earliest days Wally was always top of his school averages, always "the big noise" at cricket, always the chap whose astonishing catch had won the match.   He is of the make that never plays badly; only when it fails it is just out of form.

Not a John Tyldesley on a bad wicket—of which, by the way, our groundsmen, who have never seen Melbourne, seem to have mislaid the prescription !—Wally in form is the most destructible, devastating, masterful smasher of our bowling now in the game.

One has only to stand at slip and watch that forcer

off a stiff back leg send the ball whizzing through the cover-country to realize that here is a well-armed controller of the bat—a real player.

Weak to a leg stump attack Wally certainly was. I reveal here no secret, for which, when Kent next cross swords with Gloucestershire, he will not thank a fellow native of the former. The Australians, however, attacked him at all points on their own plate-glass pitches in 1928-29. But he made 905 runs in the five Tests all the same! Only to watch another pulveriser of bowling, Don Bradman, beat that figure by 69 runs a year later on our wickets.

Like all batsmen who came into Test cricket post-war, Hammond was, to that extent, lucky. For nobody will ever persuade me that either bowling or captaincy, or all-round fielding ability, either here or in Australia, has at any time since the war been as good as the best standard of some years before the war.

As a bowler Hammond has, in my presence, turned the ball from the off at a good pace on the Oval. That, in itself, is no mean accomplishment.

He has the correct bowling action, indeed technically one of the very best I have ever seen. Therefore one upon which youngsters should model themselves.

In addition, Hammond is a high-class fielder in any position. His name and fame as a fielder depend mainly on his results in the slips for Gloucestershire where, when Charlie Parker was in his prime, Wally's path was rather an easy one.

How easy is shown from the fact that he made 10 catches in the slips in one match in 1928, in which year he made 76 catches, which I take to be the world's record for any fielder, not the wicket-keeper, for four and a half months' cricket.

In his earlier days Wally would have been an ace among cover-points, as he has the knack of placing his hands in the right place, and he was then a quick starter.   But perpetual positioning in the slips neither adds to a man's briskness nor to his throwing powers.

Altogether, there is little joy in Kent over the fact that such ability is "wasted" under another banner ! But we applaud him all the same.


## D. R. BRADMAN.

The kind of genius batsman who arrives about once every twenty years or so on purpose to show us which really are the best bowlers !

Absolutely untaught, Bradman's success seems to make of coaching a waste of time !

Though he often plays with a cross bat, Bradman is the grandest living example for youngsters to copy in one particular.   He really *hits* the ball.

Such vicious striking at the ball as his is, and always has been, rare.   I have never seen fiercer.

As in the case of all geniuses, he exercises some kind of hypnotic influence over the bowler.   Otherwise they could not fail to more persistently attack his off stump with the going-away ball than any of them do.

No batsman can cross-bat that one for long.

In the opinion of many, he won the duel with Larwood on Australian wickets in 1932-33, and it is a great pity the renewal was avoided, when the Australians met Notts in 1934, by Bradman standing down and Larwood being unfit.   Those who hold the view that Bradman won this duel four years ago can point to his average of 58, the highest average on either side in the rubber, and to the fact that he got a hundred in the first Test he played in against the intensive leg-side attack.

I cannot write about Bradman as a batsman when the ball is turning, as I have never seen him in such conditions.

It is most remarkable and, so far as I know, commented on here for the first time, that, to date, his career has struck a dry cycle of years.

I am unaware if he has ever had to bat on a Melbourne "special"—the world's worst—but his path in England in 1930 and 1934 was the reverse of a "sticky" one.

A highest class field anywhere.

## W. H. PONSFORD.

What a lot more runs this prolific run-getter would have made, to be sure, if there was no leg-stump !

Perhaps none of the world's biggest scorers has been out so often as "Bill" through walking too far across and missing the leg-glance.

A much more stolid batsman than his famous rival Bradman, "Bill" seemed to require more digging out, as, except the stroke already alluded to, he did not chance his arm or give the bowlers anything like the encouragement that Bradman gives. But of the two, most bowlers would prefer to bowl to Ponsford.

A sound but not showy outfield, Ponsford always has been.

## HAROLD LARWOOD.

Is one of the three fastest right-hand bowlers of my time, Mr. N. A. Knox and E. A. Macdonald being the other two.

Larwood is the most accurate one of his pace I have ever seen.

That is why I have always held the opinion that there was never any need for him to play the part allotted to him on the Australian tour of 1932–33. It was not worth the risk entailed. Once it was seen how it endangered the relations between the two countries it *should have been abandoned forthwith*. Even at the cost, if that was the stake, of the rubber.   There are other things to consider besides winning.

Larwood gets his effortless pace from his muscular hips and back, and his easy swing of a long arm.   His is not a perfect action, because he delivers almost chest square to the batsman, and his bowling hand does not come from behind his back.   Both of these are definite bowling faults, but, in his case, neither depreciates his pace nor his accuracy.

There is in him the making of a really good batsman, and he will always be a good field.


## A. P. FREEMAN.

Comes of a cricketing family, two of his cousins having played for Essex, while an uncle, besides being in his day a useful player himself, has had few equals as a caretaker and maker of a first-class wicket. Witness the perfect pitches for many years at Leyton.

I do not think I have anything new to write about such a well-known and popular chap as "Tich."   Like the proverbial brook he seems to go on and on for ever, occasionally getting a rest when taken off from one end to be put on at the other.

Grumble ?   Not he.   He just hitches up his breeks, using both forearms for this purpose in a manner characteristically his own, and continues to wheel his arm over for another twenty overs or so—if our opponents last so long.

When I say that "Tich" has been useful to Kent since the War, I mean it with all my heart.   What we should have done without him it is not possible for me to put into words.   His records are too well known to need repetition here.   His first great one was to eclipse, as regards figures, the late Tom Richardson's magnificent feat of having taken over 1,000 wickets in the course of four consecutive seasons.   But in justice to Richardson, it should always be remembered that he did his achievement with five-ball overs.

"Tich" Freeman is often spoken of as being a googlie bowler. Strictly speaking he, like Grimmett with a totally different flight, relies almost wholly on the leg-break ; of which what is called the top-spinner but which is often only a leg-break that has not "bitten," is the first cousin. A leg-break which has failed to "bite" results in the ball going straight on after pitching. An unwary batsman, or one who is slow with his change of stroke, is often caught napping in this way and is out leg-before-wicket. Freeman gets his fair share of such results, and does so because of his splendid length. Length has been the backbone of his bowling, needless to add. Such records as he has made are unattainable without systematic, almost monotonous, length.

"Tich" has always been a smart little fielder in positions fairly near the wicket, and many a time he has played a most useful stubborn innings. As a bowler he is best on a drying wicket. I have written elsewhere of one of his remarkable Test match innings, in Australia. From no tail-ender have I ever seen a better.

As he is only 47, I hope to field slip to him for at least another decade. By which time there's no knowing what the Laws of Cricket will be like.

But if they have included the leg-side in the (N.) l.b.w. law "Tich" will head the averages for the rest of his life.


HERBERT SUTCLIFFE.

Here is surely one of the finest big match cricketers England ever produced.

That is not the same thing as to suggest that Sutcliffe is only a Test match or a Yorkshire *v.* Lancashire

E*

batsman. Quite on the contrary, he can be just as formidable an obstacle to the success of, say, the Toowoomba XI as he is with his ears back and Australia bowling "all out" at the Oval.

I am not of the party who suggest that because his dour methods were such an excellent foil to the rapier play of Jack Hobbs that Sutcliffe owed everything, in Test cricket, to Jack. A moment's thought should serve to show that the fielding side finding Jack in form *would concentrate upon the other end*. Thus making Sutcliffe's job the tougher. That certainly happened many a time, and cricketers know how magnificently Sutcliffe "saw it through" on many a difficult occasion.

Elsewhere in this book I have recorded my fully considered opinion that Sutcliffe should be first choice for the next M.C.C. tour to Australia, provided he is passed muscle-fit. In doing so I do not presume to dictate to the selectors of the team, but merely I voice a cricketer's opinion just as I would if I was asked for it by any selector. As, I may add, I have been frequently asked in the past.

Specially do I refer to Sutcliffe's muscle-fitness because here is a player about whose body-fitness nobody conversant with the careful, almost austere, life that Herbert lives has ever the least doubt about that. In this respect he has been all his cricketing life a model for all cricketers. Yorkshire's No. 1 looks at present like being still here in 1946. Lucky Yorkshire.


A. D. Nourse, Senior.

A very stolid left-hander, with immense hands and powerful forearms. At his best he took a great deal of digging out. Had his timing been the veriest trifle better he would have made hundreds more runs, but he "killed" the ball so often when there might have been fours.

With such hands he did not catch the ball in the slips, he engulfed it.

With the new ball and his round-arm delivery he often got good wickets owing to his very late swing.

Off the field Dave was one of the most amusing chaps I ever came across, splendid company at all times.

## S. J. McCabe.

As he is only 26, this New South Walian, who seems likely to be a captain of Australia in the years to come, has nothing like arrived yet at his best. Except for health reasons, I hazard the guess he will be a thorn in the side of the England elevens of 1938–1939–1940–1942, comparable to Trumper and Bradman, though in sedater, more stolid, style.

McCabe's off-side is very strong. and his bat very straight. He can hook with the best, and his square cut is a crasher. A useful field without being brilliant, his bowling is quite commonplace out-swerve stuff that batsmen should know by heart. But, in contradiction to many other so-called opening bowlers, he does not "play the batsman in." The difference between the two types of new ball bowlers is subtle, but well known to players.

Against McCabe a batsman has to play ; against the other kind he knows that it is only a question of time how long the shine lasts, and the bowler does not, while he himself remains.

## The Nawab of Pataudi.

As I was concerned in the coaching of this Mahommedan Prince, who, at the time I am writing, is to captain India against England this year, after having played for England in Australia and at Nottingham, my pen has the curb on.

I endeavoured to train his batting before he went to Oxford, and at a time when I hoped he would one day be in the Kent XI. That project fell through, and as the cricket world knows, he qualified and played for Worcestershire, with some irregularity of appearance.

Possessed of a good eye and wrists, the Nawab was fine material to work on. He is a natural player of ball games, very nimble and light on his feet, for which reason he should be a better fielder than he is. But in that branch of the game he did not have the same avid interest that he displayed in batting. Could it be that his aim was to do in the Varsity match that which the two famous Hindu Princes, K. S. Ranjitsinhji and his nephew K. S. Duleepsinhji had not done, and that is to score a century? If that was his goal, he achieved it in downright fashion.

In 1931 Mr. A. T. Ratcliffe made the first 200 innings in the Varsity match when he scored 201 for Cambridge. As the Nawab of Pataudi passed the other batsman at the pavilion wicket in Oxford's second innings he said: "Leave it to me," and proceeded to make the record score for this match of 238 not out.

Not satisfied with that, he equalled the feat of both K. S. Ranjitsinhji and K. S. Duleepsinhji in scoring a century, 102, in his first Test match, at Sydney in December, 1932. This actually beat K. S. Ranjitsinhji's record, as his 154 not out was made in the second innings of his first Test, at Manchester in July, 1896, when he made 62 in the first innings. K. S. Duleepsinhji's 173 was made in the first innings of the 1930 Test at Lord's.

A sound stroke player, when the Nawab means business on a good pitch his wicket is a problem for any bowler to solve, because he knows how to bat. But I must stop!

HEDLEY VERITY.

The best slow left in England for some seasons, Verity may not yet have reached his best. Like all Yorkshire bowlers who are any good, Verity knows how to place his field, and how to bowl to it. *The secret of Yorkshire's* 18 *Championships.*

Verity should be, and probably will be yet, a much deadlier bowler on hard wickets than he has proved to be of late. He has concentrated on defensive bowling too much when the wicket is very good.

Rhodes and Blythe used to produce splendid analyses on the plumbest of wickets against quite as strong batsmen as any Verity has ever had to bowl to. With such command of length as he possesses, Verity's hard wickets results should, and I think will, improve.

It's there—and will out. Let us hope on the next Australian tour, when, as things seem to me now before the beginning of the season of 1936, England's bowling outlook is definitely gloomy.

A very sound tail-end batsman, because he holds straight and has self-control.


G. G. MACAULAY.

Was one of the greatest right-hand medium fast bowlers in my experience. He was tireless, and as hostile as any bowler I ever tried to oppose. Even when I was well in and "getting 'em," he gave me no rest. I always felt I was being attacked by more than one bowler at the same time.

While George was more famous for the precision of his off-break, which was the ball that gave me most exercise, he could bowl the genuine googlie faster than any other Englishman of my time. A bowler who never gave in, he won many a game for Yorkshire because of that spirit.

He was a much better bat than is generally known, and was such a keen cricketer that he could not field badly.

The type of which Champion County elevens are made.

## S. F. BARNES.

On the principle of the finest plums being kept to the last, the reader finds the greatest bowler of them all at the end of my little Thumbnail Gallery.

Sid Barnes must be tired of hearing and reading himself described as the greatest of all bowlers.  To be sure, that is a tall order.  But I expect he has got over the monotony!  From the time he was discovered by Mr. A. C. MacLaren, who took him, a quite unknown bowler, to Australia in 1901–02 on the last tour that was run before the management of our International cricket devolved on the Board of Control, Barnes never looked back.  As showing the strength of Australian cricket at that time, England won only one Test, Australia four, although Barnes had 19 wickets for 17.00 each, John Gunn 17 wickets for 21.17 each, "Charlie" Blythe 18 for 26.11 each, and Len Braund 21 wickets for 35.1 each.

Collectively these are practically as good as bowling results as those obtained on the last M.C.C. tour in Australia, which read : Larwood 33 for 19.51, Verity 11 for 24.63, Voce 15 for 27.13, and Mr. G. O. Allen 21 for 28.23.  The four best 1901–02 bowlers took 75 wickets for 24.85 each ; the four of 1932–3 took 80 wickets for 24.87 runs each.

Yet the 1932–3 side won 4 out of 5 Tests, completely reversing the results achieved by its predecessor of thirty-one years.

The correct pitching of the fast-leg break by Barnes was perhaps the factor which first attracted Mr. MacLaren.

But that one was far from being the only shot in Sid's well-filled locker. He had a beautiful, enduring action, one of the most graceful I ever saw in a bowler so hostile and so capable. His almost natural leg-spin caused the ball always to tend to swerve in towards the batsman ; that in itself inducing "playing inside," which to any good length ball pitching on middle and leg is fatal when that ball is as likely as not to straighten, if not actually to turn towards the off, on pitching.

Add to this deadly characteristic the attacking temperament of this bowler, who, as I saw frequently from the slips, hid his intentions from the batsman, and the devastation which Barnes could, and did, spread in the ranks of thoroughly accomplished batsmen stands explained.

Barnes had more perfect control over the ball than any other bowler of my time.

Bowling both leg and off-breaks, both in and out swerves, maintaining length, and pitching a yorker almost at will, Barnes was at a modest estimate four or five bowlers in one.

If a slip-fielder keeps awake he can tell better than anyone on the field how and why the batsman was out. From my vantage point I have never noticed in the case of any other bowler so many batsmen so utterly lost as were many who had been bowled, as Clem Hill used to say, "base over turkey" by Barnes.

With my doughty partner in several tight corners for Kent, Arthur Fielder, Barnes helped to win the second Test of the 1907–08 tour, under Mr. A. O. Jones, at Melbourne by one wicket, Barnes 38, and Fielder 18 not out ; but Sid goes down to posterity, in my opinion, as the greatest of all bowlers.

It is said that third times pays for all. Barnes visited Australia three times. On each of his first two visits Australia won 4, England 1 Test, but on his third visit, 1911–12, England won 4, Australia 1.

His Test bowling figures in Australia and the total result of the 15 Tests on his three tours, there are, in my opinion, a monument to the strength of Australian batting in 1901–1912.   His figures were :—

|         |    | O     | M   | R    | W  | AV.   |
|---------|----|-------|-----|------|----|-------|
| 1901–02 | .. | 138.2 | 23  | 323  | 19 | 17.00 |
| 1907–08 | .. | 273.2 | 74  | 626  | 24 | 26.08 |
| 1911–12 | .. | 297   | 64  | 778  | 34 | 22.88 |
|         |    | 708.4 | 171 | 1727 | 77 | 21.98 |

English cricket, now in sore straits for the lack of Barnes-class bowling, would revive like magic if a bowler of anything like his ability was to arrive now on the scene.   We can only hope for the best, remembering that cricket is a game based on surprises, and that history repeats itself.

# CHAPTER VIII

### BATTING LORE

Success in first-class cricket depends almost entirely upon the individual himself.

I am afraid that in making that statement I may disappoint some people who expect that the regular perusal of the daily literature of the game, followed by a course of coaching by it does not matter what coach, will result in the production of a First-Class Cricketer.

Who the coach is matters a great deal.

Those of us who have borne the heat of the day, and have sweated with every measure of profusion under every kind of sun, from the Turkish bath type at Brisbane to the pale orb of Bradford or Manchester, know well that achievements out on "the middle" are not necessarily attainable as the result of being coached by the first coach available.

All of us cricketers are not necessarily good judges of cricketers or of the game of cricket. That proposition I lay down as being tantamount to a fact. With which only those of us who are not very strictly honest with ourselves will disagree. Some men, and not always very capable cricketers themselves, are very capable judges of the worth of other cricketers.

I have always held the view that only a good judge of a cricketer can either write intelligently about the game, or coach at it.

The greatest coach I ever had anything to do with, the late Capt. William McCanlis, of Kent, was never himself a great player. But a better judge and coach of the game, of its requirements, and its players, surely never breathed. He had the natural gift of being able to sort the wheat from the chaff. One could always be sure that if he "spotted" a promising young player then that youngster had cricket in him.

"Be natural" is the first advice, to both the youngster who would bat and to the coach who is trying to shape the first steps of his almost too attentive young charge. For although boys will be boys, and most of them are erratic and careless with the carelessness of boyhood, there are many who are too desperately serious for words. These imbibe every word their coach utters, and saturate themselves, at probably the most receptive time of their lives, with every word of advice he gives, be it good, bad, or shocking.

Thus, if the coach happens to be an unsound one the damage is irrevocably done before the youngster gets anywhere near Big cricket. I see this every year. From my comfortable perch in the slips—sometimes not quite so comfortable, since only last July, in trying to make the simplest of catches, I sustained one of the most painful injuries which participation in cricket has to offer, and that is a fingernail almost removed ; this, too, off a slow, medium-paced bowler !—I have had a close-up at one time or another of practically every batsman in first-class cricket. Nobody can tell more about the foot movements of a batsman than can an habitual first or second slip. In match after match I see batsmen, some of them over thirty, batting the wrong way, after starting by standing the wrong way !

While our lack of class bowling has been pronounced, some of our batting has been so irresolute directly the opposition has been able to produce really Good Length and Spin, that our batting is just as responsible as our bowling for this depressing inability to win Test matches during the last two years.

To lose is little, to be outclassed as sometimes we have been is quite another matter.

What, it may be asked of me, is the chief thing wrong with our batting ?

Just this.

PLAYERS DO NOT USE THEIR FORE-FOOT ENOUGH, NOT BY SEVENTY-FIVE PER CENT ENOUGH.

They bat almost as though they are one-legged men, with a fore-foot of wood !

Strong back play has no stronger votary than myself, for I know well the runs it has brought me, but in the absence of good resolute use of the fore-foot which I see annually it is almost as though Englishmen had forgotten how to play cricket !

I do not propose to go into as much detail as other and better pens than mine have done with regard to how to hold the bat and where to plant the feet—plant is perhaps the right word here, and should be well understood in some cases where the feet seem to have taken root !

My opinion is that the most comfortable grip of the bat handle is the best ; and the most comfortable stance is the best. Provided always there is nothing radically wrong with either.

The exaggerated Two-Eyed Stance with, for example, a right-handed batsman's left shoulder pointing anywhere but towards the bowler, or, at the most, towards mid-on, is utterly unsound and prevents the production of the best results against any bowler *who knows how to bowl*.

The right-handed batsman's right toe should be pointing either squarely towards point, or behind point towards "gully"—never towards cover-point.

In fact, *bat sideways*, as that grand South African batsman, Herby Taylor, says in this book.

Nobody has ever convinced me of the necessity for a batsman to contort his neck in order to have his forehead facing the bowler.

He will not add one four to his season's total, or one

per cent to his season's average by such physical manœuvres—believe me. On the contrary.

Because a grip and a stance suit me is not a reason why the same grip and stance would have suited Clem Hill or Mr. F. G. J. Ford, or would suit my friends Philip Mead or Maurice Leyland. Sutcliffe has a considerable and well-deserved record in Test cricket, as the world knows. But would any coach go out of his way to advise a youngster to use Sutcliffe's grip? I know that if I used it I'd seldom make twenty runs in an innings! But, obviously, it suits Sutcliffe, and that is all—the Individual, you see—that really matters.

You follow me, I hope? In cricket, as elsewhere, one man's meat is another man's poison.

Admitted, then, that you have quite decided to give yourself the best chance by being natural, as regards your Grip and your Stance, then your next Law of Batting is to firmly convince yourself when you shape to face the bowler, whether he has just done the hat-trick or not (even more so if he has, because, by the law of averages, he cannot go on taking wickets *every* ball) that you are just as good a bat as he is a bowler. In other words, that he has yet to prove that he is your master.

Therefore, if possible first ball, land him one to be going on with!

In most coaching too little attention seems to me to be paid to the respective mental attitudes of the two parties to this eternal duel. It has been for far too long a custom that the batsman *must* necessarily play steadily and potter about to find the pace of the wicket, to get accustomed to the light, and so on. How many "fours offered on a plate" have I seen rejected because of that too hard and fast unwritten law! There are naturally many occasions when a batsman should go slow, find himself, at the start, but there are also many when he has just gone in when he should treat a half-volley, or a long-hop pitched off the wicket, as it should be treated. I can but write of my own methods which I have never changed in thirty years. It is just as easy to get out having a crack at a long-hop after you have made 200 as it is attempting the same stroke at the same ball in the first over. The first over stroke cannot well be unsound, foolish, bad, and all that, if the other one is not. As a matter of strict cricket fact both are the correct stroke for the ball.

Here may I point out that batsmen play *strokes*, not "shots." There is no such thing as a shot in cricket, except when a fielder has a "shot at" the wicket.

Concerning this matter of the correct stroke for the ball, I will now describe what actually happened in one of the earliest matches I played in for Kent. I think I learned more that day than on, perhaps, any other one day of my whole career.

Mr. C. B. Fry, as he was then, was batting, and the wicket at Canterbury was such that, although we bowlers could turn the ball at a fair pace, the pitch could not be said to be really difficult. Over and over again I would bowl a ball pitching about on the leg or leg and middle, expecting a catch in the slips. As regularly as I pitched one more or less the unplayable length Mr. Fry would *draw away slightly* to the leg-side, *leaving his wicket open*, and the ball would go over the top, or outside the off stump.

The snick to the slips never came !

After this had gone on for some time I asked Mr. Fry about it. As he always does where a fine point in cricket is concerned, he readily gave me his views. I cannot remember his exact words, but the general sense of them was this.

When a slow left-hander is bowling on any pitch that is "doing" something, the *really* dangerous ball, and that, too, for slip catches chiefly, is that which pitches on or about the leg and middle stumps at a good length.

"I have a theory," said Mr. Fry, "that this ball, when it 'bites,' very seldom hits the wicket. It generally rises enough to go over the top. Therefore, as such a ball cannot be driven, or cut, or played to the on-side with any safety, why do the *only* thing whereby you *can* be out off it, which is, to play at it more or less blindly and get the touch the bowler is angling for ? Therefore, draw back quickly after *having watched what the ball is doing after pitching*, and let the wicketkeeper return the ball to the disappointed bowler !"

Since that object lesson at Canterbury I have often noticed the same characteristic *on that kind of wicket*.

There is no doubt in my mind that Mr. Fry is perfectly right. The safe stroke to that ball, in the conditions stated, is to make no stroke. I wonder how many coaches teach this way of playing what cricketers know as the "left-hander's ball" ?

Another tip which I offer as a law of batting, and that is : "Never *jump* in to drive." I am a firm believer in the walking-in or two-steps method of getting sufficiently near to the pitch of a slightly over-tossed ball— and, yes, also to a good length ball, if runs are wanted quickly—to really hit it. I am not conscious of ever having "jumped" when playing this stroke, of which that most accomplished player, George Gunn, was such a master.

The best, the only, way to play it is to bring the back foot quickly round behind and to the side of the fore foot, and then repeat the same step with the other foot.

One vital result of this really gliding gait is that your eyes remain on the same level all the time. Whereas, if you have pranced in, rather after the manner of a weight-putter about to putt, your eyes have wavered up and down according to the height of your jump.

It is a normal happening with the jumping-in style that the jumper often deceives himself. He does not really advance as far as he thinks he has, or as he intended to advance. Consequently he "hits short,' and either misses entirely or skies the ball. Cricketers often say of a man who jumped in only to be stumped that he just went up in the air and came down where he started from! I would never coach any youngster to favour the jump-in method. It is such a simple matter to practise the "two-step" method off the field of play, in your bedroom even, though for the sake of the crockery and electric lights, without a bat!

Another most important matter is the way you lift up your bat preparatory to making your stroke. I maintain that this should be done straight back, as nearly along the line of the middle stump as possible.

By doing this you can scarcely fail to bring the bat back again, either for a defensive or for an offensive stroke, also on the line of the middle stump, or near it. By not uplifting your bat straight back you compel yourself to make a *secondary* movement of the bat before you can deal properly with your greatest enemies, which are the Straight Ball, or the good length breaking ball which has turned after pitching so that it will hit the wicket. Capt. McCanlis was always very insistent on avoiding having to make a *secondary* movement of any kind for any stroke. He argued: "While you are doing something *which you need not have done* the ball is beating you, therefore why do it?"

Concentrate therefore, while the bowler is running up, on lifting your bat straight up back on the line of the wicket. Thus making the best beginning for a stroke.

Now, though I am a firm believer in sound back play, without which no batsman can ever expect to arrive on the top rungs of Cricket's rather long ladder, I am going to deal with what I regard as the most important aspect of the Drive. That which I am about to write applies equally to the standing still, fast-footed Drive as to the Drive made after the batsman has walked in to get nearer to the pitch of the ball.

For I will never admit a player as having been pupil of mine, either actually or through the medium of this book, who *jumps* in to drive. On that subject I have just said all I have to say. I will deal now with the footwork necessary to make the perfect Drive.

It is a simple matter, and therefore quite easily acquired by anybody who cares to persevere. It is just this.

That the position of the fore-foot of a batsman who has arrived at the moment when he makes his hit *must not be square across the line of the wicket,* that is to say, with the toe pointing towards cover-point.

The toes of the fore-foot *must* be pointing more or less straight up and down the wicket.

The reason for this will become at once obvious to anyone who makes both attempts a few times, and who notices carefully what happens to his knee-to-hip muscles and to his follow-through in both cases.

With the fore-foot square across the pitch those muscles go taut, there is a distinct checking of the stroke, and practically no follow-through.

When the toes are almost straight down the wicket, comfortably so, of course, there is no checking of the thigh muscles and the follow-through is fluent and sweet ; in fact, it is the natural outcome of swinging a bat as hard as one can for the purpose of hitting a ball.

Here let me advise every young reader to make a habit of *really hitting* when playing the Drive. There is in most of our big cricket enough and to spare of timid, gentle tapping of the ball.

If driving, why not drive ?

Quite whole-heartedly, and furiously enough so that you, at any rate, think you can hear the "Whoo-sh !" of the blade.

I am convinced that the emptiness of our out-fields and the repeated placings of "silly" points and mid-ons that we see to-day is not the result of so-called "spot" bowling by the dozens of medium to slow-paced bowlers now in the game, as is often alleged to be the case.

"Silly" points are *allowed* to stand there, on true hard, run-getting wickets, too. Medium to slow bowlers are *allowed* to bowl without anybody deeper than deep mid-off because of the incompetence of so many batsmen where Driving is concerned.

I am quite ready for any criticism that may come to me for writing it when I write that the same bowlers who get away with it to-day on hard wickets, with their "silly" points and untenanted straight and off-drive fields, would have cost their side an average of about three fours, at least, per over *with their to-day's setting of the field* had they bowled before the War.

I do not except one of them, unless it is Grimmett, whose command of the ball has been always marvellous, and possibly O'Reilly.

Batsmen like Commander Fry, K. S. Ranjitsinhji, John Tyldesley, Mr. K. L. Hutchings, Mr. G. L. Jessop, Mr. Percy Perrin, Mr. A. C. MacLaren, of course Victor Trumper, Charlie Macartney and Jack Hobbs, and not forgetting George Hirst, Mr. Sam Day, Mr. C. J. Burnup, and Mr. Jack Mason in double quick time would have made these "silly" positions absolutely untenable.

That I am not drawing a fancy picture is shown by the fact that though Hirst was himself one of the toughest and best of mid-offs who ever played cricket, he confessed that whenever Mr. Hutchings came in he, Hirst, always moved a few yards back at mid-off !

I have been told that when Mr. Perrin made his 343 not out against Derbyshire both the Derbyshire fast bowlers, Warren and Bestwick, who were quite as fast as anybody bowling in first-class cricket last season, had four fieldsmen in the deep field for him. But his driving still produced the record number of fours hit in a first-class innings, viz. : 68 !

In no cricket that I played in during my nine seasons before the War did I see "silly" points, short-legs, and "silly" mid-ons in such profusion as I have seen them during the past, say, ten seasons. Most of these post-war seasons happen to have been on the whole hard wicket ones.

I regard the frequency with which to-day these "silly" fieldsmen are posted, and the immunity they enjoy, as the most convincing and final evidence of insufficient use of the fore-foot in our batting as a whole. If batsmen used that foot much more, and swung freely on to it the ranks of the "silly" fielders would simply disappear.

The correct use of the "silly" positions is on soft or drying pitches when the ball is "talking," or, cocking up unexpectedly, and is not coming to the bat as it does on firm surfaces. From the day that batsmen make more of a habit of walking in to the pitch of the ball, or of hitting harder as a habit when they do hit, from that day the "silly" points will cease to be so "silly." They, and their captains, will become sensible in a night.

So far as my personal experience of them goes, I cannot say that I ever took special notice of these "silly" people. Like everyone who ever played in big cricket, I suppose I have been caught by a "silly" fielder, and no doubt shall be again—but I have a kind of subconscious recollection of having also caused most such inquisitive folk to get back a bit.

I remember that in one Test Collins persuaded Tommy Andrews to stand there to me. He did not remain after the third ball. I took four off it—the ball going somewhere between his shins.

Having had my say about the Drive, I deal now with the Cut—that most beautiful of all strokes.

If there is a stroke which is at once more pleasing both to Mr. Striker and to Mr. and Mrs. Spectator, and all the little Spectators who understand a good thing when they see it, than a firm well-hit Cut, then, I confess I do not know it.

There are two ways of making the Cut, either off the fore-foot, generally flung across on the line, or just outside it, of the off-stump ; or off the back-foot moved back on the line of, or beyond, the off-stump.

Of these two the first is infinitely the more risky, the more flashy, but certainly the fiercer. A well-timed fore-foot Cut, properly hit with the blade centre, never gives the field a chance unless it goes straight to one, when he has no doubt about it, unless he misses the ball altogether, that he has been playing cricket.

The back-foot Cut is the one which should always be played if there is time for a preference. Though I must admit that the batsman has not got much time in which to make up his mind, let alone to change it, once either Cut is decided upon.

The reason why I recommend the back-foot Cut is because the player has his eyes more facing the ball all the way than they can ever be in the case with the other Cut.

Thus, he is better able, after years of practice, I may add, to place the ball clear of fielders than he is in the case of the fore-foot Cut, which cannot be other than more or less a blind slash at a ball whose advance he has been watching over his shoulder.

These two strokes, the Drive and the Cut, cover practically the whole of the offside and the area behind the bowler on both sides of the wicket. Not until you are very adept at both can you expect to be able to "place" either stroke with any degree of accuracy to beat the field, which is supposed to be placed for the express purpose of preventing you from scoring fours. Therefore, do not try to swim before you have learned to walk properly by attempting fancy strokes for the purpose of avoiding the fieldsmen before you have mastered the way to make each of these strokes in the correct way. Then, by degrees, you will find that you will place the ball more or less instinctively.

"Placing" cannot be taught. Be sure of that. It is born of a precious sense of locality, of being able to remember where each fieldsman was *when you last saw him* before you concentrated on the bowler and the ball.

For this reason wise fielders at cover, mid-off, mid-on, "gully" and in the "blind" positions at short-leg and leg-slip do not remain rooted on the actual blade of grass upon which they were stationed by the bowler, or the captain. All these fielders should be allowed to use their own judgment to a certain extent, so long as it is understood that in doing so they do not wander yards from where they were put.

The late Mr. A. O. Jones, greatest of all gully fielders, never remained glued to one square foot of turf. He watched his victim—and his bowler—until the victim never knew where he was ! That is the way to become a great fieldsman in certain positions, though not in all.

Hence it is absolutely essential to the most profitable way of playing the Drive and the Cut to take your bearings before each ball is bowled. Doing so photographs on your mind the position of those fieldsmen who matter most, and in course of time, with long and intent practice, you will find that your hardest hits send the ball, as it were, of its own accord to places where there is nobody to field it ! In other words, you "find the gaps" which exist in every field, and thus acquire the reputation of being a batsman for whom it is difficult to place the field.

The best of that kind I ever saw was K. S. Ranjitsinhji, although my experience of his batsmanship is not an extensive one. I have always been told that Dr. Grace was supreme at placing the ball but I never saw him, nor the equal of that almost uncanny batsman who everybody, whether they knew him or not, always called "Ranji." Batsmanship can scale no

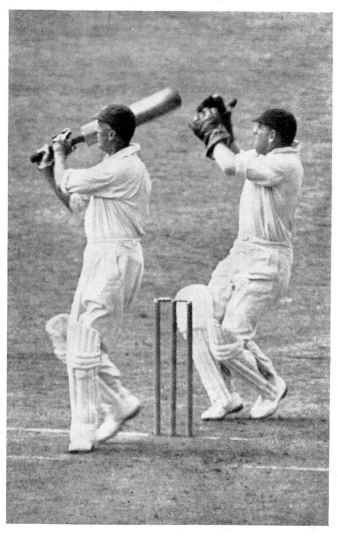

OUT OF THE OVAL!

A six "hooked" on to the tram-lines in Harleyford Road, during
my 229 for Kent at the Oval, July 27, 1935. My fore-foot is
swinging round, helping the stroke

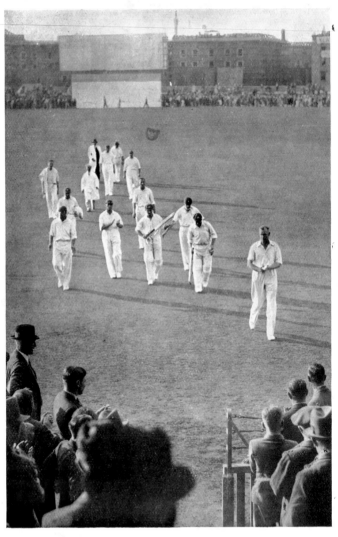

THE END OF A PERFECT DAY!

W. H. Ponsford leaving the field at the Oval, August, 1934, with
over 200 not out in his pocket.  He was out eventually "hit
wicket, b. Allen, 266," having helped to add 451 for the second
wicket with Bradman, "c. Ames, b. Bowes, 244"

higher summit than the accurate placing of hard hits on the off-side on a turning wicket. That I have seen "Ranji" do, so I give him the palm, without reservation.

Next come Victor Trumper, J. T. Tyldesley, Mead and Jack Hobbs. I have never seen Macartney or Bradman on a "sticky dog."

On-side batting plays a great part in the game nowadays. The mere fact that so many runs are scored on the on-side is something of a reproach to the bowling because, strictly speaking, the only really *safe* strokes on the on-side are made off either too short or off overtossed deliveries. In other words, off bad length.

Really good length straight bowling—a different length, that is, for each batsman according to his height and his methods, is *always* difficult to score off on the on-side. That must be obvious to everyone. Hence the deduction from this enormous prevalence of on-side play that we see that too much bowling nowadays is neither straight nor good length.

The *safest* method for run-getting on the on-side is to move the back foot as far back towards the stumps as you can safely do without breaking the wicket, *after you have seen the ball in the air*, and have been thus able to judge instantly what is its probable length. The back movement must not be begun, as I fear the average modern bowler has allowed too many batsmen to do, *before* the ball is bowled.

This is the most common fault in modern batting, and it is responsible for many of the frequent complaints about dull and slow cricket.

Because the habit is productive of so many half-cock dead-bat strokes, which are the bane of the spectator.

In that sentence I think I have put the root cause of dull cricket in a nutshell. An over of this kind of batting is a clear case of nothing doing, nothing done. Neither side is a bit better off at the end of it, unless the batting side happens to be obliged to play to save the match. For which unavoidable state of affairs there is no cure in our three-day cricket.

To decide our matches on the first innings, here let me say, does not seem to me to be the cure. If that rule is ever brought in the result would be anything but cricket. It would be only some new form of exercise, and not worth playing in. I have seen too many brilliant and thoroughly sporting recoveries to have any doubt on this point.

*Having seen the ball* and decided that its length will be too short to play forward to, or to drive, the back foot must be *instantly* moved back and the lower hand slipped down the bat handle simultaneously ; while the uplift is as straight back along the line of the wicket as possible. The back foot must go back in front of the stumps, how much in front varying according to the direction of the ball, which, let me emphasize, is almost of as much importance to the batsman as its length.

The chief thing to do is to get into the best position to be *over* the ball. Obviously, if you have seen that its direction is several inches outside the off-stump it would be foolish to step back on the line of the leg-stump. In such case step back on the line of just outside the off-stump.

This is particularly necessary now in view of the (N) l.b.w. law, wherein the part of the batsman that is struck must be "between wicket and wicket." If, therefore, you have stepped outside the off-stump and the break on the ball beats your bat and hits your outside leg you cannot be out under the new rule.

But the stepping back action is not done with a view to defeating the l.b.w. law.

It is done because it is the correct—the only— stroke to play. He is an incompetent batsman who cannot play it effectively. The action does not in any sense come under the heading pad-play.

When the player has positioned his back foot correctly, the toe pointing towards cover or mid-off *when on-side or leg-side play is intended,* he will find his fore foot has followed suit, and that his body is on the swing round towards the on-side. This is as it should be, for it helps to give more force to the stroke, and does not prevent the player from keeping well over the ball should it tend to "go-away" instead of coming on to the bat.

Assuming that it is an off-and-middle or middle-and-leg ball of fairly good length not short enough to hook, the actual stroke must be timed so that just as the connection is made between bat and ball the lower hand, taking command of the bat, turns the blade over so that its face faces short leg, delivering a pushing or glancing blow at the same moment. This stroke yields runs anywhere between forward short-leg and fine leg according to the pace of the wicket and the ball. The greatest accuracy in timing is necessary here to avoid playing the turning stroke too soon, thus causing the edge of the bat, broadside on, to meet the ball and offering a catch-and-bowl chance.

The hook, which is part of on-side play, can only be played to a much shorter pitched ball than the one I have just been writing about. This may be played after either moving back the back foot or advancing the fore foot slightly, but generally the former. The batsman's chest is practically square to the bowler when the ball is hit with the lower hand often almost down to touching the bat shoulders. The ball should be hit to either side of deep square leg.

The pull is a totally different stroke from the hook, though the latter is often described as a pull. The pull is played when the batsman flings his fore foot out almost at full stretch and hits right across the line of flight of a ball pitching *off the wicket* on the off-side. If the (N) l.b.w. rule becomes law—as is, I think, certain—the pull will tend to go out of fashion, because, in making it, the batsman's legs are almost always between wicket and wicket and the ball is an off-ball. Before (N) came in, if the ball was missed at an attempted pull and it hit the batsman he could not be out.

Another profitable on-side scoring stroke is the leg-glance, which is played only at fast or fastish balls pitching on the line of middle and leg, or leg or just outside the leg-stump. The batsman plays slightly forward but with the bat-blade facing forward short leg, great care being taken to play accurately up and down the line of the advancing ball. Its pace, if the batsman's stroke is correctly timed, does the rest. In playing this stroke great care must be taken not to play across the line of flight of the ball.

The correct stroke is *straight forward*, and by that road fours are certain—in fact, against the right kind of ball, money for nothing.

I have gone right round the circle now from the Cut to the fine Leg-Glance. The rest is with the young reader, who must all the time Think Cricket, and, when he has thought a lot, begin to think over again.

As Capt. McCanlis said, one is always learning, so there is plenty to think about. In this respect I am reminded of the remark of a very famous trainer who was talking about his apprentices. Said he : "Gordon Richards has got where he is because he thinks racing while he is riding, and he thinks about it when he isn't riding. Now, if my apprentices who think about the pictures when they are at the cinema would only not think about the pictures when they are riding a race, they'd all the sooner emulate Gordon." I commend this for absorption by cricket colts, wherever they may be.

# CHAPTER IX

## BOWLING AND FIELDING

ABOUT bowling I will be brief, because you cannot become a first-class bowler by reading about bowling.

The combined wisdom of Barnes, Mr. F. R. Foster, Rhodes and Grimmett welded together in one chapter of cold print would never produce a Test bowler out of one whose bowling lacked natural flight, and whose temperament lacked the concentration necessary to master length and spin.

Young bowlers can only improve by their own hard work, but if their bowling lacks flight and length—never mind about spin and swerve—they can never hope to get out of the "also rans."

Grip the ball in the way that suits you best and begin by constant practice at pitching the ball straight, and then a length. To do this you must bowl for hours at a single stump to get straightness. If at the same time you place a mark less than five yards from the stump and combine your attempts at straightness with attempts at hitting the mark all the better.

Never mind at first about either break or flight. Those are in the higher regions of bowling.

If you have flight naturally, all the better for you, for although the way to flight a ball may be learned to a certain degree, there is no substitute for an action which of itself causes a deceptive flight.

The best grip for the plain straight ball at the single stump is with the first and second fingers on either side of the hidden seam of the ball and therefore at right angles to the raised seam. A ball so held and released without turning the hand or fingers right or

left will travel towards the stump spinning truly backwards towards the bowler. It *should* go straight on
after pitching, any deviation from the straight line
being due to some inequality in the ground. This part
of the arduous job of learning to bowl is a long and
hard one, some might call it monotonous. But it is
never that for any youngster who is really keen

The next step after having acquired a certain ability
at bowling both direction and length is to be able to
pitch a spinning ball on the length mark. The grip
for the off-break of a right-hand bowler is with the
first finger as nearly as possible at right angles across
the raised seam of the ball. The other way round, of
course, for a left-handed bowler's natural break. The
rest of the ball lays in a kind of recess formed by the
thumb, the second and the third finger. At the instant
of release the ball so held must be spun over from
left to right, or for a left-handed bowler from left to
the off-side (in which case it will be a leg-break to a
right-handed batsman). A ball so spun will turn on
pitching from the off if bowled by a righthander and
the wicket is taking spin.

For a leg-break a right-handed bowler places the
ball in a cup formed by either his first three fingers
and thumb, or, as a few bowlers do, by using only the
thumb and first two fingers. In this case at the instant
of release the fingers and wrist working together spin
the ball from right to left, that is to say, from the leg
towards the off-side. Such a ball pitching on a "biting"
wicket will turn from a right-handed batsman's leg-
side towards his off-side.

The bowler must persevere with this ball until he
can bowl one ball straight at the off-stump without
any off or leg-break spin on it, and then bowl the next
ball with leg-break spin on it to pitch on the same spot
as the ball before.

When he can do this at will he can call himself a
bowler—but not until.

The object of this manœuvre is to make the batsman edge the second ball to give a catch in the slips because, thinking it is a plain straight ball, he will not allow for leg-break when playing his stroke and, therefore, will play inside the ball.

Similarly, an off-break bowler must persevere so that he can bowl a straight ball at the off-stump and then bowl the next ball to pitch on the same spot, but this time with off-break on it so that unless the batsman plays it the ball will get past his bat, because of off-break, and go on to hit the leg-stump.

Any player who can do these two things *to order*, and pitch a good length, according to the height and reach of the batsman, has begun to be *a genuine first-class bowler*.

Another ball every youngster, and especially fast and fast medium bowlers, must learn to bowl is the yorker. I am not going too far when I state that until a fast or fast medium bowler can pitch a yorker to order he has no right to be considered to be a first-class bowler. The yorker pitches on or just over the popping crease. It is such a destructive ball that I have never met a batsman who liked a yorker on the line of his leg-stump early in his innings, or indeed at any time. It is the best ball of all to bowl to a forcing type of batsman at any time, but especially in his first over. The reason for this is that a yorker depends for its success upon being mistaken for a half-volley. Every true yorker looks like a half-volley from the batsman's end, and, consequently, the tendency is for the batsman to try to drive the ball. Thus he tries to make bat and ball meet at some spot about a yard or more in front of the popping crease after the ball has pitched. As the true yorker pitches on or inside the popping crease, it is obvious that unless the batsman sees his mistake in time he is sure to be late with his stroke.

There are two ways, and two only, to play a true

yorker. One is to come hard down on the ball as it pitches, and *hold the bat there firmly*. The other is to play straight forward, with the bat end close to the ground, and push the ball straight up the pitch, striking it *before it pitches*.

The art of bowling does not finish at acquiring the ability to bowl a breaking ball or a yorker or a well directed swerving ball. Every bowler must set his field specially *for each different batsman* and must then bowl to the special setting.

It follows from this that the bowler should know better than anybody how to place his field.

Every good captain recognizes this.

But this is not the same thing as saying that the captain has nothing to do with the setting of the field. On the contrary, the captain has the best right of all, viz., a captain's right. But every good captain, recognizing that the bowler who knows his job knows best what field he wants, invariably leaves it to his bowler.

I know that Mr. MacLaren, on putting Blythe on, would say, "I want you on now at the top end, 'Charlie' —you know how you want your field, put them where you like," and the game went on smoothly. Without long and unnecessary delays caused by the captain waving his arm about moving one man four feet six inches one way and another on to the next blade of grass to the one he was standing on.

Mr. MacLaren held the sane cricket view which may be best expressed by this question : "If 'Charlie' Blythe doesn't know where he wants his field, what's he doing in the England eleven at all ?"

While claiming for the bowler the right of first say in the placing of his field, I am obliged to say that this right does not in the least justify him in refusal to bowl unless his field is placed exactly as he desires. That road leads only to controversy and disaster.

The captain's wishes in this matter, being tantamount to an irrevocable order, are paramount. Nothing else matters, nor ever did, in a well-ordered cricket team.

Bowlers sometimes know better than their captains. That is an undeniable truth of first-class cricket. Especially in those cases where the captain does not happen to be a bowler himself. It is in such cases that damage may have been done to the interests of the eleven in the field by the—shall I call it ?—obstinacy of a non-bowler captain in imposing on his bowler a setting of the field which the bowler himself did not want.

Rubbing a bowler up the wrong way is the best way not to get full value out of him.

As I do not wish to rub anyone up the wrong way, I quote the following instance, suppressing the names of the principal actors on purpose. I write of what I saw and heard myself, so this is no second-hand tale.

A left-hander was bowling to a left-hander. He placed two short-legs, as the wicket was doing a bit, only one slip and a backward point. With the obvious hope that his leg-stump and middle-and-leg attack, with the break turning the ball in on to the bat, would sooner or later bring about the short-leg catch which is part and parcel of cricket when two left-handers are having a duel. After a couple of overs of this the captain, a non-bowler, went up to the bowler and said :

"Put a second slip, bowl him the one with-the-arm, and no more of that muck."

This, although the wind was useless for the one with-the-arm, while the wicket was just about right for the off-break.

When, later, the captain changed the left-hander—who, by the way, had not got a wicket he said : "When you get back to —— you can tell them you've *at last* had your field properly placed *for you !*"

I refer to this case as it is the one exception to a rule I have seen broken only on this occasion that relations between captains and bowlers on the field are harmonious and have been always conducted in a friendly and sportsmanlike manner. In my opinion, the captain in this instance was wrong from start to finish, both as regards his treatment of his bowler as well as in the interests of his side.

When a captain considers that one of his bowlers is not perhaps concentrating, the normal way to bring about a change in his methods is for the captain to put it in the form of a suggestion. That brings prompt response and willingly attempted execution from any bowler worth his salt.

One more matter of importance regarding the setting of the field, which as it concerns captains as well as the bowler I refer to before I turn to the art of fielding. This is the slavish placing of deep-square leg fielders on a soft or turning wicket for a slow or medium paced left-hand bowler.

Such a bowler is not worthy the name if, in such conditions of wicket, he needs a deep-square leg.

It is an open confession of incompetence, or lack of ability to control the ball, if on a soft or turning pitch a left-hander posts a deep square leg. If he bowls accurately the very absence of a deep square leg will get him wickets. The posting of a deep square leg leaves an unnecessary gap elsewhere and is, for that reason alone, bad cricket.

Now for Fielding.

This summer I hope to succeed in making at all events six catches in order to complete my 1,000—perhaps even in May !—therefore, as I have got so far, I trust I may be considered qualified to write about fielding.

The first essentials are untiring alertness, backed by quick eyesight, quick movement, and very sensitive fingers and palms.

The high-class fieldsman must be, indeed is, something of a juggler, a sleight-of-hand artist.

The fact that fielding is largely a gift which cannot be acquired is proved by the form of such artists as Mr. G. L. Jessop and Hobbs. If ability at cover-point can be learned, how comes it that, in spite of incessant attempts by countless cricketers, the ability of these two has never been equalled?

We have not now got even one youngster in his twenties so good as Hobbs was at cover when past forty.

That depressing fact, however, must not be allowed to act as a wet blanket. Rather should it be an incentive to further and greater endeavour, on the strength of the truism that there are as good fish in the sea as ever came out of it. Since my young readers may take it from me as gospel that neither Mr. Jessop nor Hobbs, magnificent natural fieldsmen though they were, kept their form without incessant practice. They were always flinging the ball to the wicket-keeper in order to maintain the accuracy of their return.

After all, pianists and riflemen practice without ceasing, yet our cricketers expect not to become rusty though they do as little practising catching and fielding as possible!

Though you may not all become like Hobbs or Bradman in the field, you can at least try to be so.

The best way to begin is to live with a cricket ball. Carry one about with you.

Be spinning it, and catching it, and chucking it to your best friend and he flinging it back to you, as often as you can. Both in and out of the cricket season. By thus making the grasping, the feel, of a cricket ball part of his daily routine, any youngster can improve his fielding out of recognition.

There is no royal path to unfailing success out on the field.

If all catches were held, the county cricket clubs would all be bankrupt in a few seasons.

Let me give an instance of what can happen, because

this did happen, in a county match. Kent were playing Warwickshire on a private ground at Birmingham. The pitch had been covered all over, but at one end the rain had got through the cover so that we got what we call a "hot and cold 'un," dry and fast one end and softish at the other.

Whether the different paces at which the ball left the ground at the two ends was the cause or not, we, of Kent, put fourteen catches on the floor before lunch.

In all my experience I never saw anything like it. Mr. A. J. Evans was our captain, and another subsequent Oxford captain, Mr. G. B. Legge, was in the slips with me. I believe he put the first one down. Wright at mid-off missed three, one after the other. "Tiger" Smith, who made 150, was dropped certainly seven times, and Bates, too, was let off two or three times. After about the seventh was laid on the grass, Mr. Evans sang out to Mr. Legge in the slips : "Come on, Geoff, out of that, I'll field next to Frank." Within three overs Mr. Evans had missed two ! I could not help laughing, whereupon our skipper said : "Hanged if I can see what there is to laugh at."

Presently Wright remarked to Mr. Legge : "Frank's not dropped one yet."

"He will presently," replied Mr. Legge.

Sure enough, two overs later, "Tiger" snicked one past my ear for four. Of course, I ought to have had it, but Mr. Legge burst out laughing, half afraid of Mr. Evans, now in the gully. He was by now thoroughly fed up, as he said : "You fellows are always laughing when you ought to be serious."

To which I replied : "You know, sir, about that epidemic, don't you, the one that's not catching ?" and the incident, which had begun to look awkward, ended in chaff all round.

But, seriously, it was the most amazing hour or so's cricket in my experience. Unless one had seen, and shared in it, it would be impossible to believe such a series of misjudged catches possible on the part of normally quite useful fielders.

A few tips on the subject of what fielders ought to do and I will end.

SLIPS.—*Stand still*, feet apart, and watch the ball from the bowler's hand. First slip, stand clear of the wicket-keeper so that you can reach with your left hand the snick that he cannot reach with his right. Second slip, stand slightly in front of first slip and so wide of him that, when both have your arms outstretched there is a space of at least two feet between the tips of your fingers. Third slip, similarly in relation to second slip. The three slips should never stand in a straight line but on a curve.

GULLY.—About eight yards, or less, from the batsman and five from third slip. *Watch the batsman's feet* until he has decided on his stroke, then his bat. Stand still, flinch at nothing, and take what comes to you. It won't come slowly.

THIRD MAN.—Almost directly in line behind gully, and expect every ball to curve to your left hand. If the ball has been cut hard *and straight* there should never be a second run. If it has been cut, or snicked, wide of you there is always a second.

COVERPOINT.—Watch the batsman's feet while you are walking in quickly to *every* ball bowled. Expect every hit along the ground to curve to your left. Always throw your return to the wicket-keeper full pitch, aiming at his throat. If you aim at his hands the ball will reach him a yorker, when the "four for overthrow" will be your fault.

Never throw at the stumps except as a very last resource, or when the batsman's wicket is worth the risk of an overthrow.

MID-OFF.—Practically the same rules as for coverpoint except that the ball only rarely curves to your left. It does so if it has been sliced and not truly hit.

F*

LONGFIELDS.—*Never stand on the edge of the boundary*, always a few yards inside it. Most hits drop the ball several yards short of the boundary.

It is one of the greatest, and most common, of fallacies that it is more difficult to catch a ball when the fielder is running backwards than running forwards.

The reverse is actually the case. As can be seen by a glance at the respective positions of the fingers and palms when running in towards an advancing ball, or when running back.

THE THROW.—This is one of the most important, as well as one of the most neglected, branches of the whole business of fielding. That regular players, and especially coverpoints and outfields, do not practice enough is certain.

The first rule of throwing is : "When within your range, *always* throw a full pitch, preferably to the wicket-keeper."

To whom you throw is governed always by what the batsmen, both of them, are doing. So that it is bad cricket to lay down the law that the ball should be returned to the wicket-keeper. Unfortunately, most bowlers are slack about getting back to their wicket, and many captains have either not the personality or the command over their men that is necessary in order to drill bowlers into performing this first duty once the ball is delivered. Consequently, fielders, outfields in particular, have become mechanical—as though there is any place at all in cricket for mechanism !—and throw by force of habit always to the wicket-keeper. Batsmen with their wits about them soon get to know the slaves of this bad habit—and the score then benefits by easily taken singles. There are in fact some outfields to whom it is "always two."

All throws from the outfield should have low trajectory. Outfields who throw high are either unfit or too old for the job.

The higher the throw the easier the run.

*I have never seen anyone run out from a high return.*

The long distance throw should always be made with the greatest violence of which the thrower is capable, the ball being hurled so that it reaches the wicket-keeper or the bowler *first* bounce. That is the method which yields run-outs, and it should be for that reason alone mastered by everyone who fields "in the deep."

Unless an habitual deep field can throw *with low trajectory* first bounce to the wicket-keeper standing behind the stumps, at least 110 yards distant—a throw rarely needed on any of our grounds—then that fieldsman cannot consider himself in the first class.

Outfields must make a point of finding out for themselves which is the faster runner of each pair of batsmen, so that, about ten yards before they reach the ball, they will know which is the right end to throw to.

THE WICKET-KEEPER.—The best have the least flourish, and make the least noise.

These last two seasons all young England that went to the Test matches saw the two finest modern exponents of the art—Oldfield, and the late very much lamented H. B. Cameron. To "keep" like they did should be the aim of every aspirant to fame with the gloves.

The best stance is the most comfortable one for the individual concerned, but there are three things which the keeper *must* observe.

He must stand just so far from the off-stump and on the off-side of it so that the wicket is within easy reach.

He must never snatch at the ball, but let it come to his hands, which by instinct and practice will position themselves.

He must never move his feet *backwards*—to the leg-side, yes, and occasionally his off foot to the off-side, but backwards never.

Many wicket-keepers stand about a yard too deep for their fast bowlers. The result is that they have to take the ball too often down at their toes, instead of knee or shin-high.

But a very serious fault I have seen of recent years in our county cricket is that of wicket-keepers who desert their post and walk in towards the ball which is being thrown in from the outfield. In all such cases it is the wicket-keeper's *first* duty to keep the stumps between him and the thrower. The only case in which the wicket-keeper is justified in deserting his wicket in order to run towards the ball is when a chance exists —and he the only fielder within reach—of a run-out at the bowler's end if he dashes out, fields the ball, and throws to the bowler.

Otherwise, the wicket-keeper is a soldier on guard at one spot, and one only. He must sit tight there, not even going far to one side or the other to try to stop a bad return, unless he *knows* there is nobody backing up.

There was a time when it was held to be part of the wicket-keeper's duty to chase the leg-side ball, but now that there are normally as many fielders on the leg-side as on the off—Ames tells me that on the last tour in Australia the off-side was like a desert !—these stern chases, which always used to delight spectators, and in which particular phase of the game my sturdy little friend, Bert Strudwick, holds all the records, have practically disappeared from the game.

More's the pity, because any move in the big game which specially interests the faithful public that keeps it going, and which tightens that bond of sympathy between it and the players which means so much to both parties, is all to the good.

The mere sight of a wicket-keeper galloping after the ball—perhaps racing mid-on for the right of returning it—all arms and legs, shedding a glove here, his hat there, and crowning all by going a proper purler just when the prize seemed to be in his grasp, has often turned the mood of an otherwise humdrum afternoon's cricket into a thing of joy and banter for the rest of the day. Cricket can ill afford to lose any such merry unrehearsed moments.

# CHAPTER X

## MY WORLD'S XI

IN this law-ridden era in which we live there is the satisfaction of knowing that no law can ever be framed to prevent one from being one's own selection committee.

That, at all events, is a very satisfactory condition of affairs from the point of view of the apparently never-ending numbers of public selection committee men.

When I first began to play in the big game it was a rare thing for even an accredited critic of cricket to announce to the world what would be his England Eleven. Still less did members of the public write to the papers to proclaim their views on the same topic. Judging from the experiences of the last few years, all was well only in those days! Because nine-tenths of the recently published unofficial elevens would not have got very far when tested by the only proof that matters, which is that of play out on "the middle."

One such team, I recall, was minus a wicket-keeper, another had four fast bowlers and only one man who had ever stood in the slips!

However, I am going to exercise the right of every individual and lay myself open to the wind from every quarter of criticism by stating that My World's XI, chosen only from men with and against whom I have played, would be sent in to bat in this order:

Victor Trumper (Australia)
Jack Hobbs (England)
K. S. Ranjitsinhji (England)

John T. Tyldesley (England)
Charlie Macartney (Australia)
Mr. J. R. Mason (England), Captain
Mr. F. R. Foster (England)
Harold Larwood (England)
Bill Oldfield (Australia)
Sid Barnes (England)
Colin Blythe (England)

I must confess that I should not expect My XI to beat the following team with confidence overflowing to the extent of planking down a large sum of money in order to back my fancy. But cannot the same thing be said about any World's XI as compared with the next best ?

Here is the "second" XI that would, I think, make a match of it with mine :

Mr. A. C. MacLaren (England), Captain
Commander C. B. Fry (England)
G. A. Faulkner (South Africa)
D. Bradman (Australia)
W. R. Hammond (England)
M. A. Noble (Australia)
W. Rhodes (England)
H. B. Cameron (South Africa)
J. M. Gregory (Australia)
E. A. Macdonald (Australia)
C. V. Grimmett (Australia)

I give Trumper and Macartney the preference over Bradman as I have not seen Bradman get scores after rain, and he has not yet had the class of bowling to compete against that both the others had. I have in mind also the flawlessly straight bats of Trumper and Macartney and the occasionally very cross bat of the present idol of Australia. Bradman is not a better field than were the other two in their respective positions, and, in fact, is not so good as Trumper was in the deep field. Trumper could throw well over a hundred yards, and his return from the "deep" was always quicker than the more leisurely but otherwise perfect return of Don. I am not suggesting that Bradman cannot throw in fiercely from the outfield, as I have seen him do it. But, well, I have my preference, and have stated it.

Trumper's superior for certainty of scoring off the good length ball—the supreme test, this, of batsmanship—I have never seen.

On our wickets Philip Mead in his best day was very good indeed in this way, but he had, of course, never the graceful agility and ease of Australia's greatest batsman.

Trumper was a beautiful player. He raised batting higher than anyone else I have seen. He, if anyone ever did, made of it a physical fine art. What a pity he was born too soon, and there is therefore no cinematographic record to show the world in slow motion how graceful a man can be when wielding a cricket bat.

In a much more sedate way our own Willie Quaife was the nearest approach to Trumper in this matter of perfect execution. I did not see the late Mr. Lionel Palairet so cannot give my own opinion where is his place among batsmen to watch whom was a sheer pleasure.

Trumper's movements were to batting what those of Sid Barnes were to bowling. A more beautiful, though hostile, action than that of Barnes I never saw. I cannot see how it could have been improved upon. The more sinuous, limpid swing of Mr. F. R. Foster was almost clumsy, for all its smoothness, by comparison to Sid's. A great and workmanlike pair these two, so opposite in style as well as angle of delivery, and such attackers, both of them!

Friendly opponents of My World's XI may pick and choose and sort and sift where they like. I defy

them to name, as a pair, a better than Mr. Foster and
Barnes among bowlers of my time, 1906–35.

The wicket-keeper ? Well, P. W. Sherwell of South
Africa, "Dick" Lilley, England, and H. Carter of
Australia take a lot of leaving out ! Aye, they were all
three of them good 'uns.

I wonder which, the old hands, say a committee
composed of Messrs. Jackson, MacLaren, Fry, Jessop,
Noble, Armstrong, Hill and Trumper, would choose if
they were asked to decide which of Lilley or Carter
knew most about cricket and his own particular job in
it ? I leave this point for pavilion discussion, and
carry on.

I have chosen Oldfield because he is so good, at his
best, at taking every kind of bowling and, important
thing, he has such a straight bat. Cameron kept
magnificently all last season, and was a high-class
batsman but, judged by the Test class standard, he
was not a *safe* batsman. He was almost too brilliant
for Test cricket !

Thus, whereas in, let us say, a series of ten Test
matches Cameron might be backed, and Oldfield certainly not, to hit a brilliant hundred and fifty, it is a
sure thing that the last-named would have had the
higher average, and would have played more "utility"
innings than his South African rival. Both are right
up high in the first flight among wicket-keepers, and
must be worthy successors of such great men of the
past as Blackham, Halliwell, Pilling, Lilley, Sherwell
and Strudwick.

Mr. Jack Mason. He was a greater all-round
cricketer than the world ever knew, and was enor-
mously popular. I know that the best leaders are not
necessarily the most popular ones, but, if we of Kent
have a voice in cricket, I know I am speaking with it
when I say that the Kent XI, who knew Mr. Mason
better than anyone, would have done anything for
him. In My World's XI he adds appreciably to the

bowling strength, and helps to strengthen it in what I recognize is its only weak spot, the slips.

Mr. Mason was a very fine slip fielder, though I must own that he and K. S. Ranjitsinhji, as the late Jam Sahib of Nawanagar was when I started playing, and Mr. Foster are not so strong a "set" of slips as would be Mr. MacLaren, Hammond and Gregory of the opposing team.

My "third man and out" positions in the case of Trumper and Tyldesley is stronger than that of the opposition, Bradman and Commander Fry.

My sticky wicket batting—Tyldesley, "Ranji," Trumper, Hobbs, Macartney and Mr. Mason—is, I think, better than that of Messrs. MacLaren and Fry, and Bradman, Noble, Hammond and Faulkner.

In fielding I think that of these two teams My XI certainly has the vote, and neither side has anyone to "hide."

In bowling, which would you rather have to bat against, Foster, Barnes, Larwood, Blythe, Macartney and Mason, or Gregory, Macdonald, Rhodes, Faulkner, Grimmett and Noble ?

I should not strap on my pads bursting with confidence against either set.

So I conclude this chapter with the comforting remark that we are all lucky in that none of us has ever had to, or can ever have to, cope with such barrages.

# CHAPTER XI

## LOOKING AHEAD

CONSCIOUS that the very title of this chapter envelops me, whether I like its pattern and cut or not, with the mantle of Elisha, I will finish my book by writing what is in me, letting prophecy take care of itself.

I do not attempt to forecast the future wherever I now mention a cricketer, and I am quite prepared to find in after years that some about whom I write have not made the necessary improvement which must be taken for granted whenever one writes or speaks encouragingly about the form of a comparative young-ster at the game. Health, business, or home worries, or a temperament that is perhaps not sedate enough to ensure prolonged success at a most exacting game, each and every one of these things may falsify any cricket Elisha.

It is scarcely possible without living cricket with the player of whom one writes to make more than a guess at his games-playing temperament.

I must crave, therefore, the kindness of my reader when I express an opinion about the possibilities in the cricket of anyone who is not a member of that little Kentish family which is known as the Kent eleven.

Before, however, I embark on writing about the future of individuals in the cricket field, there is some-thing which I should like to say about the existing state of affairs as it concerns the control of the game. I hope I may do so without being considered guilty of presumption. The role of Dictator would not suit me at all.

From time to time a bit of a stir is made in the

Press or in pavilions—I regret to say only when England has just lost, or is not winning, a rubber—on the
subject of the age or the unsuitability for other reasons
to control cricket, of the gentlemen who give so much
of their time to service on our Board of Control, or
on the Committee of M.C.C.

My opinion on this matter, which I venture to offer
because professional cricketers are naturally concerned
in it, is that not on any account would I vote for a
change from the established order of things.   That
order may not be faultless.   Is any human institution
without fault ?

In this matter the most important thing for the
general public to realize is that the game of cricket
can only be governed by cricketers for cricketers.  Any
attempt to control it on the lines of professional foot-
ball, for example, would end in confusion and disaster
in no time.

Taking the above mentioned three governing bodies
in their reverse order, the M.C.C., being a private club,
its committee is no concern of non-members.   For
them to suggest the type of man who should serve
on the M.C.C. Committee is merely impertinent.

The Selection Committee is in different case.   It is
an offshoot of the Board of Control for Test matches
at Home, to give the Board its full title.   This Board
was formed in 1898 and cricket has to thank Lord
Hawke for it, as it was at his instigation the Counties
requested M.C.C. to bring it into being.

The constitution of the Selection Committee, which
places the National Eleven on the field, is certainly a
matter of keen public interest.   But it is not elected
by M.C.C., and is not answerable to M.C.C., which has
no more to do with who plays for Engand than has
the man in the moon.

Because of this Committee's responsibility for the
National Eleven, it is not surprising, perhaps, that a
few of the more venturesome members of the public

consider they should have some say in who should and who should not serve on it. Nevertheless, I do not admit the public's right to enter into this matter at all. I am of that opinion because if, as, only when England is losing, the public critics generally protest, the Selection Committee is unfit for its job, by what reasoning can the public, which does not travel about daily watching players, and the vast majority of the members of which have never played in a first-class, let alone a Test match, be regarded as qualified to adversely criticize the work of first-class cricketers who have the necessary qualifications for the job? By the very criticisms they make the public critics of the Selectors prove that their own knowledge of the game is immature, and in some cases quite negligible.

The charges which are most often levelled at the Selection Committee are :

(1) That they are not active cricketers ;
(2) They are too old ;  and
(3) That only those cricketers actually regularly in county cricket are fit to serve as selectors.

Dealing with these charges in their numerical order :

(1) I know that active cricketers have quite enough on their hands to captain their county elevens without having to worry about fitting together Trial teams, and attending meetings and so forth, in the middle of county matches,  Where, for example, would it be convenient to Messrs. Chapman, Sellers and Holmes to meet if Kent were playing at Dover, Yorkshire at Hull, and Surrey at Weston-super-Mare ?

Or do the objectors to the present system expect the county secretaries in the autumn to dovetail county matches so that on an unknown Sunday in July or August next three captains shall be playing within easy reach of each other ?

Furthermore, it is a well-known fact that county

captains are, and have rarely been otherwise, very loth to press the claims of their fellow county players when the time arrives to choose the England side. A prophet has scant honour in his own country.

Serving on the Selection Committee would be looked upon with anything but joy by most county captains, or else I have been playing in county cricket all these years with my ears closed.

(2) I do not see that age has anything to do with it as long as the selector *is a good judge of the game*, who is physically able to get about. At the age of eighty, Capt. McCanlis's judgment, for example, might have been taken as the equal of anybody's on any question of cricket.

I cannot see, either, why if older men make mistakes younger men should be infallible.

(3) For reasons given in commenting on (1) I do not think that active cricketers are the best suited for service on the Selection Committee.

A glance at the record of Selection Committees for the whole period of Australian visits, only since I came into first-class cricket in 1906, is, I find, informative. In the names of selectors, that of the chairman is put first, and that of an active cricketer is in italics.

| YEAR | COMMITTEE | RESULT OF RUBBER |
|---|---|---|
| 1909 | Lord Hawke, *Messrs. C. B. Fry*, H. D. G. Leveson-Gower | Lost |
| 1921 | Messrs. H. K. Foster, *R. H. Spooner*, J. Daniell | Lost |
| 1926 | Messrs. P. F. Warner, *P. A. Perrin*, A. E. R. Gilligan | Won |
| 1930 | Messrs. H. D. G. Leveson-Gower, *J. C. White*, F. T. Mann | Lost |
| 1934 | Sir Stanley Jackson, Messrs. P. A. Perrin, T. A. Higson | Lost |

It will be seen that only the 1909 Selection Committee was made up of cricketers who were all still playing in first-class cricket.

The last two committees, including here that of 1935, still in office, are the only two Selection Committees all three members of which are retired cricketers.

Last season's committee chooses the teams against India this year, and if asked by the cricket committee of *M.C.C.*, not unless, will help in selecting the team that is due to go to Australia in September next.

The above facts give scant support to the theory that the selectors should be active cricketers.

They do, however, tend to show that the presence of professional cricketers on the Selection Committee is a good thing, because England's only rubber won out of these five was won when Hobbs and Rhodes were co-opted in 1926. But I think it is rather generally admitted that in the fifth Test at the Oval in that year, which England won and with it the rubber, rain and hot sun just before Australia's second innings were not unlucky for England, and may indeed have been the deciding factor.

On the question of whether professionals should be selectors, I prefer to keep an open mind, and to refrain from expressing a more decided opinion than that I think that, on the whole, professionals—especially when they are actively engaged in the game—would prefer to be excused the duty of having to vote a brother professional out of such an honour, with its attendant financial considerations.

But, at the same time, I should be inclined to regard a professional who has had Test match experience and who has retired from the game as a very suitable man to act as a selector, provided he is not an umpire.

The main point is to get good judges of cricket, who can spare the time to see the best players all over the country, to serve as selectors. But even when England wins I reckon it must be a rather thankless job, and not a cure for insomnia.

I come now to the consideration and the naming of some of the most promising young players, judged from the *standard required for Test match cricket*, whom I have seen during the past two or three seasons.

I am sorry that professionals predominate in my list, just as they do in the county elevens of to-day, because if there is one thing about which I really feel sure about the future of the game it is that an increase in the number of amateurs in every county eleven is an immediate and a crying need.

Beginning, like charity, at home, I name Arthur Fagg (20) and Leslie Todd (28) first. I have great hopes of both playing, and doing well, for England in the near future.

Fagg's batting is sound and he is a good field anywhere. He can keep wicket and is a keen learner.

Todd is already a good left-handed batsman, not a negligible bowler, though he will be a better one as soon as he has obtained more control of length. He is a simply magnificent field anywhere. I unhesitatingly include him in my next Sixteen to Australia.

Another grand fieldsman who would be one of my first choices for Australia is Arthur Mitchell (33) of Yorkshire. This is a batsman with the straight bat and the sticking temperament needed for play-to-a-finish cricket. Typically Yorkshire, the tougher the fight the happier is he. A brilliant fielder anywhere, perhaps even the quickest all-round fielder we possess, it is not possible to name a position that Mitchell would not fill with distinction.

T. S. Worthington (30), of Derbyshire, is an all-rounder of a sound type of whom I hold a very high opinion. I regard him as a sound player who has not yet received his full recognition in representative cricket.

Derbyshire has two more extremely promising

cricketers in the brothers Pope, of whom A. V. is 26 and G. H. 24. Fine tall fellows, both have the makings of extremely good—I might even risk the word great —bowlers. Unless something happens to check normal progress in their case it is, I feel, not going too far to say that this pair might one day create record by being the first brothers to share the bowling for England in an Australian Test match.

In writing this I must plead guilty to not having been present when the great Dr. W. G. Grace and his two brothers, E. M. and G. F., played for England at the Oval, so I am unaware whether any two of them have forestalled me.

The Popes seem to me to possess something in their bowling which I have noticed only in the bowling of great bowlers. Perhaps A. V. is the better of the two, but beyond that I will not go, except to say that they cannot afford to do anything now but persevere hard if they desire the highest honour cricket has to offer a professional.

I do not see how Mr. R. W. V. Robins can be omitted from the next tour. Strictly speaking, he is not the "safe" type for Test cricket, and, to be sure, his is a three-day and not a play-to-a-finish style. But such a thoroughly capable fielder, who can bowl the unplayable ball as often as anybody now in the game, and a hard wicket batsman, who is only 29 years old, simply has to be included. Indeed, on all-round merit nobody can exclude Mr. Robins from England's eleven and again hold up his head as being a judge of the game.

Bob Gregory (33), of Surrey, is on my list—but only as a No. 4 batsman. He is not, in my estimation, a one of a first pair player. A good slip or outfield, he pulls his weight in any team he plays for.

Another who I mark as highly probable is Mr. C. T. Ashton (34), of Essex. Here is a grand cricketer. The very type that should do well on Australian pitches.

His is the cricket temperament which any Test XI would welcome.

C. Washbrook (20) is one of the most likely youngsters that Lancashire has shown us since Ernest Tyldesley. This boy has a great future, if he observes Capt. McCanlis's rule and "is never too old to learn." He is quite a good field.

As I have a strong belief in the value of all-rounders in Test cricket, I place Nichols (36), of Essex, unhesitatingly before Bowes in any Test XI, whether for an Australian tour or in English Tests. If both were at the top of their bowling form, perhaps Bowes would achieve the better analysis in a given match, but as that cannot be guaranteed I maintain that Nichols' good slip fielding and left-handed batting ability weighs down the balance in his favour as against Bowes. Nichols is a good attacker, moves the ball in the air more than Bowes does, and has more control of it.

I was much impressed with the bowling at Dover of Pollard, of Lancashire, but I do not think he is as yet quite ripe for Tests. This type of bowler, however, sometimes arrives with a bound right in the first flight. I do not exclude him from the Sixteen, nor can I place him in it.

Mr. A. B. Sellers (28), the Yorkshire captain, is already, in my opinion, a good captain. I place him high enough to be a highly probable choice for the next Australian tour. He is a grand, keen and active fieldsman, and a batsman of whom we have not yet seen the best. He is one of the only five amateurs who made a century against the Australians in 1934, the others being Mr. Wyatt for M.C.C. at Lord's; another Yorkshireman, Mr. W. E. Harbord, for the Minor Counties, at the Oval; Mr. F. C. de Saram, of Oxford University; and Mr. A. W. Snowden, of Northants.

Since Mr. J. W. H. T. Douglas, England has not

had a more thorough all-round trier in her side than Mr. G. O. Allen (33). If he reports physically fit he is the captain of my Sixteen. Quite apart from having had Test match experience, he would be very popular with his team and, I believe, with the Australians.

A. W. Wellard (32), of Somerset, a really lion-hearted fast bowler, good field, and splendid hitter, should go on improving for a few years. Sticklers for correctness will say that he gives the ball too much air to be a Test match cricketer, but I do not altogether agree with that theory, although admitting that it has its points. A man cannot hit more than sixty "sixers" in one season as Wellard did last year without having an eye for the game.

Mr. E. R. T. Holmes (30), the Surrey captain, is a match-winner type, who has great possibilities as a captain because he is not afraid to make experiments and to take risks. A pretty good slip or fieldsman in any position, Mr. Holmes is a useful change bowler, and a stroke-playing batsman who has not yet reached his best. He is very popular with his professionals.

I was very sorry to read during the winter that there is talk of him giving up the game. I hope that in this case second thoughts will prove the best.

But for his indifferent health I would include Copson (26), of Derbyshire, in my Sixteen, but an Australian tour makes exacting physical demands on a man. I regard Copson as definitely a great bowler now with the new ball for a short spell, because he is able to make it move in the air from both directions.

That sound bat, J. M. Sims (31), of Middlesex, is England's most promising professional break bowler. Watching him, I feel certain he has studied the bowler's job. He spins the ball a lot more than many with bigger reputations as spin bowlers than he had secured before his recent Australian-New Zealand tour under Mr. Holmes. A thoroughly honest hard worker at the game, Sims should be busy these next ten years.

I wish I could see more wicket-keepers coming along to step into he boots of "Dick" Lilley, Strudwick, Duckworth and Les Ames. The best, in my opinion, of the non-caps is Cornford (35), the little Sussex keeper, who for so many years has stood up to Maurice Tate. Cornford is a thorough trier of the "Struddy" type, and I cannot pay him a higher compliment, for "Struddy" was one of the outstanding wicket-keepers of my time. Cornford is not a presentation wicket as a batsman, and altogether I must regard him as well in the running for the return ticket to Australia next September.

If Sixteen had had to be chosen to go to Australia last September, mine would have been : G. O. Allen (captain), C. T. Ashton, A. B. Sellers, R. W. V. Robins, R. E. S. Wyatt, Hammond, Leyland, Ames, Cornford, Mitchell (Yorkshire), Nichols, Todd, Worthington, Verity, Wellard and Sims.

Perhaps the best possible eleven from these men, in their batting order, would be : Mr. Wyatt, Mitchell, Hammond, Leyland, Mr. Ashton, Ames, Mr. Allen, Worthington, Mr. Robins, Nichols, Verity.

This side contains the two best fast bowlers on their day we have, Mr. Allen and Nichols, the four best proved batsmen with Test experience (excluding Sutcliffe, of whom I shall write presently) in Mr. Wyatt, Hammond, Leyland and Ames ; the best batsman-wicket-keeper, Ames ; two brilliant covers, Messrs. Robins and Ashton ; the best slow left, Verity ; two very good slips who can also bat, Hammond and Nichols ; the best all - round fielder in England, Mitchell ; two excellent third men and out, Messrs. Robins and Ashton ; and a good close-in fielder, Mr. Wyatt.

I am prepared for a good season this year by Sutcliffe. That would force this grand Test match batsman automatically into the running for a final trip to Australia.

When Sutcliffe is fit the England XI is incomplete without him.

His sedater style of 1935 may or may not be suited for Test matches in England, but I cannot regard him yet, at the age of only 41, as an exploded force for Test matches in Australia. Fit and well as regard muscles as well as body—and I know nobody who has taken more trouble over physical fitness for Test matches than Commander C. B. Fry, Jack Hobbs and Herbert Sutcliffe—there is nobody yet amongst our players who has merited precedence of choice for England's No. 1 for a tour in Australia over Yorkshire's great batsman.

I can imagine the sigh of relief out there when the team is announced if Sutcliffe's name is not in it.

It is only because he has broken down more than once for muscular causes that I have not included him in my Sixteen.

Something of the same kind may be written of Mr. C. F. Walters, that most capable Worcestershire batsman. If he has recovered his health he must be a very strong candidate for the next tour, but I am a little dubious of his staying power for the trying needs of an Australian trip, where play-to-a-finish cricket on rock-hard surfaces soon finds out any weak spot in a player if there is one.

My ideal first pair of all those playing regularly last summer is, without question, Mr. Wyatt and Sutcliffe. Mr. Wyatt is a much more valuable No. 1 than No. 5. So much so, that if Mr. Wyatt is not considered good enough as a first-pair player, then Mitchell is the one to take his place, Mr. Wyatt standing down.

I hope Yorkshire will send Mitchell in with Sutcliffe all this season in anticipation, and for the good of English cricket, which, on the next tour in Australia, will need all the help it can get at the start of every innings.

No question of how to play the new ball should be

permitted to enter here, because a No. 5, in Test cricket, has to cope with it—that, too, often when bowlers are warm and loose and flushed with success —just as often as has a No. 1.

Further, I am sure, we pay too much attention to such points as who can and who cannot play the new ball well.

After all is said and written, it is derogatory to even think of a cricketer, who has reached Test match rank as a batsman, that he cannot play a bowler who is using a new ball so well as he can play the same bowler when the ball is a bit worn.

Surely it is assumed that a Test class batsman has ability enough to stop and to score off every kind of bowling ?

My own personal view is that the task of a No. 1 or 2 batsman is incomparably easier than that of, say, a No. 4 or 5 who has got fairly well "in" on the worn ball, then to find, on the 200 being signalled, that a Gregory, a MacDonald, or a Larwood has been launched at him.

Those who have no first-class playing experience of the great difference in the bowling between 175 and 200, and that while 200 is mounting to about 240, are a little apt to waste time talking or writing about the unfitness of so-and-so to be one of a first pair.

Personally, had I the choice I would always go in first. For one reason, and a not unimportant one, because it is the easiest place in which to make runs !

My chief reason, however, for preferring Mr. Wyatt and Sutcliffe as our first pair is because the first time they partnered each other in a Test they had a hundred partnership, and Sutcliffe went on to make 194. That was at Sydney on Dec. 2, 3, 5, 6, and 7, 1932. England made 524 and won by 10 wickets.

Again, last summer Mr. Wyatt and Sutcliffe put up a hundred for the first wicket at Trent Bridge against South Africa.

There should be some very sound reason before
Sutcliffe is omitted from the next tour. A careful
living fellow like Herbert, who will be only 42 next
November, can still stay the Australian course with
ease, if his muscles are all right.

Some readers will no doubt find omissions from my
list which will surprise them. I have gone carefully
into this matter more than once and cannot find any
other cricketer who I would "pass" Test-match fit in
preference to those whom I have included.

I turn now to other matters more concerned with
the Laws and Politics of Cricket than with players of
the future. In this that which is best recognized as
the (N) L.B.W. rule comes first.

I have no hesitation in expressing the hope that
this will be incorporated in the Laws of Cricket before
the first ball of 1937 is bowled.

In its first season's trial, 1935, this rule exceeded
the expectations of those who had a good deal to do
with the launching of it. These, I reveal no secret in
cricket circles at all events, were an Oxford and a
Cambridge cricketer respectively. One a right-handed
bat, the other left-handed, both of the very highest
standard as players. They were Commander C. B.
Fry and Mr. F. G. J. Ford. It is true that the Hon.
R. H. Lyttelton had been urging an alteration to the
old L.B.W. Law for many years before them. But
things were brought to a head by the two old players
I have mentioned. The drafting of the (N) rule was
partly the work of another Old Reptonian, like Commander Fry and Mr. Ford, the former Cambridge and
Gentlemen's bowler, Dr. A. Farr Morcom.

The original proposal did not include the vital
words "between wicket and wicket," and I have not
been able to discover who is responsible for them. But
there they are, and, personally, I hope they remain.

At the same time, I hope the authorities do not spoil
their own good work by going too far and including

G

the ball pitching off the wicket on the leg-side. If that is done, the whole thing will be spoiled.

Let the Ball and the Bat share the L.B.W. mode of dismissal fifty-fifty, remembering that the leg side is the blind side of the batsman.

For obvious physical reasons the batsman cannot defend his wicket so readily on the leg-side as he can on the off.

He is always, and must be for ever, more vulnerable to the ball that "goes away from his bat"—that is to say, the ball which pitches on his leg-side and which either because of break, or "go with arm" or swerve, goes away towards the slips—than he can ever be to the off-side ball.

Therefore, I beg of our legislators never to make the mistake of including the leg-side in the L.B.W. Law.

It is not illogical to exclude it while admitting the off-side, because of the above always present and immovable reasons.

The (N.) L.B.W. rule is a thoroughly good rule because :—

(*a*) It compells the batsman to play more *at the ball ;* the habit thus formed will develop as players get more accustomed to it, and with that development greatly increased play on the off-side cannot help but follow.

(*b*) It hinders incompetent batsman from staying in and making scores above their real value ; not because it directly gets them out, but because it makes them attempt strokes which at present they know little or nothing about, not having taken the trouble to practise them.

(*c*) It tends to shorten such individual innings and therefore to finish matches ; a most desirable happening in our three-day, always time-limited, cricket ; this will be less apparent as batsmen learn to cope with the new law.

(*d*) It does not seriously hamper competent batsmen, be the wicket good, bad or indifferent, but rather on the contrary, gives them scope for proving how accomplished they are by the making of large scores in spite of this additional Bowler's Aid.

After all, a success secured after being put to the Proof of Play always silences criticism. The (N.) rule has, so far, won that success. It gave, in my opinion, a most satisfactory, even almost a conclusive answer to its numerous adverse critics when put to that proof last year.

Many who at first would have none of it, Sutcliffe for one, have changed their mind. He has admitted his mistake in the frankest possible manner.

Early in the season, Mr. Fender committed himself to the decisive opinion that it is a "Monumental Failure." I do not know whether he has since changed his mind. If he has not, he has the knowledge now that he is in a very small minority.

Not only do the South Africans, after two successive seasons' trial, strongly approve of (N.), but our own Advisory Committee of the Counties *unanimously* recommended, on Nov. 19th last, to the M.C.C. to continue the new rule in 1936. In addition to these decided expressions of approval on the part of those who have tried (N.), New Zealand, looking ahead with a vision that I recommend to the Australian Board of Control, decided last October to bring the rule in to their cricket.

Then, following the Australian Board's refusal to agree to playing it on their 1935–36 South African tour came the bombshell—for their prestige in their own country—that the three most important States of New South Wales, Victoria, and South Australia had all decided to adopt the rule. Had there been a good many more cricketers on the Australian Board than there are, no doubt there would not have been this refusal to come into line with the rest of the world of cricket.

When (N.) was passed as an experiment for 1935, all

kinds of opinions were expressed the very next day as to how it would play. One of the forecasts was that left-handed batsmen were in for a thin time because their off-side could be attacked by bowlers pitching on the "cut-up" of bowlers from the other end.

As to this I was out once (N.) in the whole season ; and I do not mind confiding to the reader, strictly in private, that when my left knee was struck on that occasion it was well outside the off-stump ! I am not complaining, still less disputing, the umpire's decision. I am only stating the fact. There will be many such faulty decisions, because it is just as impossible for the umpire to be right every time in (N.) as regards the leg being "between wicket and wicket" as it was for him to be right every time under the old rule about the ball pitching "on the wicket."

Another gloomy forecast, before the 1935 season began, was that after rain matches would be over in a day. The Proof of Play silenced that silly view conclusively, so far as one season's trial could do so. But before this point can be finally judged we must have a really rainy season, like 1912 for example. Nothing within my experience last year justifies any such view of the new rule.

On the contrary, on the "sticky dogs" batsmen will play *at the ball* so much more that I incline to the belief that wickets will be less easy to get, so far as L.B.W. is concerned, on the glue pots to come than they were on those of the past. Then batsmen chanced their arm at off-breaks, knowing that if they missed they would not be out. In future they will chance less and less.

As the results prove, the Kent XI, which, win or lose, always plays *at the ball*, was not much disturbed by (N.).

So I did not see, perhaps, as many dismissals that way as others may have seen. But, from my eyrie at first slip I observed that umpires, quite rightly, gave most decisions, when appealed to under (N.), in favour of the batsman *who had played forward.*

That is sound umpiring as regards its encouragement to play forward, and is, in my opinion, a good reading of the law. If a front leg is struck when its owner has played forward it cannot be much less than 8 feet from the stumps when it was struck.

With the aid of a piece of string it will be at once seen that a breaking or swerving ball, which had pitched a fair length even off the wicket will never hit the wicket.

It is not always remembered that the (N.) rule concerns *only* a breaking or in-swerving ball.

The above does not apply to the off-break of bowlers who are bowling round the wicket.

While on the subject of umpiring, I must express the opinion that umpiring was as good last season, on the whole, as it has ever been in my time.

It is not my place to mention names, but I must say that many of the umpires who do not officiate in the Tests are just as capable as those who do—so high is the general standard of umpiring.

Still looking ahead, another matter may be dealt with as briefly as possible as it is relatively unimportant. At any rate, in the eyes of the cricketers chiefly concerned. I refer to the crusade, blaming M.C.C. as usual—who, by the way, have nothing whatever to do with the matter—because members of the English team are not obliged to stay at the same hotel on the occasion of Test matches.  •

Speaking for myself, and for those of my brother professionals to whom I have mentioned the matter, I see no point at all in the suggestion. It carries with it two implications, which players themselves resent.

First, that although they are considered by the appointed persons to have arrived at the Test match standard as players, nevertheless they are presumed not to know what is required of them out "on the middle," and apparently cannot acquire that knowledge without going through some mysterious process known, I believe, as "getting together."

Second, there is the inference that on such an important occasion as a Test players cannot be trusted to look after themselves, but must be all kept together, under the eye, presumably, of the captain.

The mutual hotel idea might have some point if the Test was played at some unknown, never previously visited, town.

As things are, most of our Test players, having played previously at Nottingham, Leeds and Manchester, have each of them almost always put up at a particular hotel. Why should they be made uncomfortable by being obliged to stay at some other hotel for a very doubtful benefit to the playing ability of the team ? The idea certainly has some force in the case of a professional colt in his first Test. He might feel "out of it" and a bit lonely if, for example, playing at Leeds or Manchester for the first time after travelling from Taunton or Tonbridge. Particularly if he was the only member of his county side in England's team. But to me it reads as merely absurd for a Test at Lord's or at the Oval to expect Hendren, Ames, Nichols, Tate, Mr. Wyatt (whose home is in Surrey), Mr. Allen, and Mr. Robins to stay from Friday night to Monday night at a London hotel.

If the practice is to come into being on the score of the need for "getting together" it must be done for every Test, or for none.

I am not suggesting that some such arrangement will never come into force, as in these days when that valuable saying, "Let well alone" is all too often ignored, there's no knowing what may happen

I am sorry to disagree with the reformers who wish the Board of Control to make this mutual hotel business compulsory, but, quite frankly, I can see no use whatever in the idea. Except in, perhaps, the case of an entirely "new" England side, under a new captain.

It might reasonably be pointed out that the English team stayed together in the same hotels in 1920–21 in Australia and yet *lost all five Tests*.

The English Team did *not* stay together in either 1905 or 1926, *but it won the rubber, nevertheless*.

I do not know how the advocates of this formal arrangement, which, if I may say so, would make of Test cricket an even more desperately businesslike matter than it has already become, get round the results of 1905, 1920–21 and 1926 ?

The thing they advocate trespasses also on the happy family aspect of our game of Cricket. Some of us cricketers have friends who very kindly put us up when we are honoured by being chosen for England. We are glad to accept their hospitality, and they are, I know, proud to house, even if only for a long week-end, a member, or members, of England's team. All that kind of social enjoyment must go by the board at the stroke of a pen to please whom, and to do what good ? For the life of me, I don't know !

But I do feel that the carrying out of this disciplinary act would not benefit the English eleven a run, a catch, or a wicket.

When the Kent XI won the Championship it did not always stay at the same hotels either in or out of Kent. That is still the practice with us.

Players who have risen in the game to the position of being fit to be chosen for England are rightly presumed to know all that is required of them before they arrive at the town where the Test is to be played. At which I leave this subject to those with whom the matter rests.

With this last observation that if the chosen eleven is not in itself good enough to win, staying at the same hotel will do nothing to make it so.

And so I arrive at the last overs. I can sense the field glancing at the clock, and I can see the public beginning to collect their belongings preparatory to the journey home. The journey home ! Whence have you all come, you very faithful followers of our greatest game ? Often I wonder.

I remember once chancing to meet a man at an Old Trafford Test who said he'd come all the way from the Fiji Islands ! He said he'd a brother who saw me make my 305 not out against Tasmania, and his brother had "ordered" him to see "that chap Woolley the very first chance you get."

I have seen old and frail ladies leaving our tented fields in Kent as though their visit there had been part and parcel of their daily existence. At Canterbury, as I am sure at every other famous "Week" wherever these are held, there come families who wouldn't miss attending on any account. Kent winning or Kent losing, they come and they go, all the better for having spent the best part of a day in the open air watching the grand old game which has been handed down to us.

With whatever its faults, Cricket's appeal *whenever it is brightly played* is such that a man is the better for watching it.

*But the generation to come must see to it that the bat is used for its rightful purpose.* IT IS PRIMARILY A WEAPON OF OFFENCE, NOT OF DEFENCE. SEE TO IT THAT IT REMAINS SO, *and then that which the Public so rejoice in seeing, the Champagne of Cricket, will never lose its fizz.*

This burden rests on the shoulders of the Players themselves.

Rightly or wrongly, I always feel that those who have served their apprenticeship on the village green realize this rather more fully than do others who never had the advantage in this respect.

Have I omitted anything ? Well, among the goings and comings of nigh One Thousand Matches, the bowlings and catchings and stumpings of Thirty Years on the Middle, it would be strange indeed if I have missed nothing.

But omissions or not, I must now put away my pen.

For I hear Kent a'calling.

So I must pack my bag and go to begin my next Chapter out on the place that matters most—the Middle.

G*

# A FEW FIGURES

I DESIRE to acknowledge here, with the utmost gratitude to my friend, Mr. A. K. Mowll, of Dover, the assistance which his book of statistics, containing all my scores and wickets, has been to me in the production of this book.

The following figures are taken from the volume in which he has recorded my every score and analysis, from my first innings, a Duck, to my last, a Century.

As, happily, I retain the power to add to both, I hope to give him a lot more work !

## My Bag for 1906 to 1935

Number of Matches Played in.................. 922

Number of Ducks' Eggs....................... 86

Number of Centuries for Kent ................ 115

Number of Centuries in all .................... 141

Number of scores between 50–100 ............ 416

Number of catches made ..................... 994

Number of catches made for Kent.............. 863

Number of Tests *v.* Australia............... 32

                South Africa ........... 26

                New Zealand ........... 5

                India ................. 1

                         — 64

Number of consecutive Tests against Australia and

    South Africa ........................... 52

Number of runs scored..................... 54,236

Number of wickets taken ................. 2,081

## BATTING AND BOWLING AVERAGES—ALL MATCHES
### (K. signifies for Kent)

| Year. | | Runs. | Average. | Runs. | Wickets. | Average. |
|---|---|---|---|---|---|---|
| 1906 K. | .. | 626 | 24·45 | 842 | 42 | 20·04 |
| | | 779 | 31·16 | 887 | 42 | 21·11 |
| 1907 K. | ... | 1,034 | 28·72 | 518 | 16 | 32·37 |
| | | 1,128 | 26·85 | 623 | 21 | 29·66 |
| 1908 K. | ... | 1,120 | 32·00 | 1,017 | 58 | 17·53 |
| | | 1,286 | 29·90 | 1,355 | 80 | 16·93 |
| 1909 K. | ... | 922 | 31·79 | 1,063 | 57 | 18·64 |
| | | 1,270 | 32·56 | 1,399 | 72 | 19·43 |
| 1910 K. | ... | 966 | 26·83 | 1,630 | 124 | 13·14 |
| | | 1,101 | 24·46 | 1,973 | 136 | 14·50 |
| 1911 K. | ... | 1,525 | 42·36 | 1,388 | 70 | 19·82 |
| | | 1,700 | 37·77 | 1,814 | 85 | 21·34 |
| 1912 K. | ... | 1,104 | 42·46 | 1,329 | 95 | 13·98 |
| | | 1,827 | 41·52 | 1,802 | 126 | 14·30 |
| 1913 K. | ... | 1,507 | 43·05 | 1,462 | 83 | 17·61 |
| | | 1,760 | 45·12 | 1,542 | 83 | 18·57 |
| 1914 K. | ... | 1,933 | 46·02 | 2,119 | 112 | 18·91 |
| | | 2,272 | 45·44 | 2,412 | 125 | 19·45 |
| 1919 K. | ... | 772 | 42·88 | 1,458 | 90 | 16·20 |
| | | 1,082 | 41·61 | 2,196 | 128 | 17·15 |
| 1920 K. | ... | 1,548 | 39·69 | 2,203 | 164 | 13·43 |
| | | 1,924 | 40·93 | 2,633 | 185 | 14·23 |
| 1921 K. | ... | 1,621 | 50·65 | 1,940 | 123 | 15·77 |
| | | 2,101 | 42·87 | 2,697 | 167 | 16·14 |
| 1922 K. | ... | 1,868 | 53·37 | 2,556 | 142 | 18·00 |
| | | 2,022 | 45·95 | 2,995 | 163 | 18·37 |
| 1923 K. | ... | 1,662 | 42·61 | 1,651 | 84 | 19·65 |
| | | 2,091 | 41·00 | 1,938 | 101 | 19·10 |
| 1924 K. | ... | 1,418 | 45·74 | 1,187 | 59 | 20·11 |
| | | 2,344 | 49·51 | 1,749 | 81 | 21·50 |
| 1925 K. | ... | 1,990 | 55·27 | 1,553 | 63 | 24·65 |
| | | 2,190 | 56·15 | 1,610 | 65 | 24·76 |
| 1926 K. | ... | 1,439 | 47·96 | 1,027 | 30 | 34·23 |
| | | 2,183 | 46·44 | 1,347 | 36 | 37·41 |
| 1927 K. | ... | 1,444 | 42·47 | 702 | 27 | 26·00 |
| | | 1,804 | 46·25 | 794 | 29 | 27·37 |
| 1928 K. | ... | 2,582 | 58·68 | 905 | 32 | 28·28 |
| | | 3,352 | 61·03 | 981 | 34 | 28·85 |
| 1929 K. | ... | 1,683 | 45·48 | 796 | 36 | 22·11 |
| | | 2,804 | 56·08 | 1,133 | 50 | 22·66 |
| 1930 K. | ... | 1,823 | 50·63 | 391 | 13 | 30·07 |
| | | 2,023 | 44·95 | 530 | 16 | 33·12 |
| 1931 K. | ... | 1,659 | 44·83 | 78 | 1 | 78·00 |
| | | 2,301 | 48·95 | 99 | 1 | 99·00 |

| Year. | | Runs. | Average. | Runs. | Wickets. | Average. |
|---|---|---|---|---|---|---|
| 1932 K. | .. | 1,258 | 37·00 | 28 | 1 | 28·00 |
| | | 1,827 | 36·54 | 76 | 2 | 38·00 |
| 1933 K. | .. | 1,368 | 32·83 | 6 | 0 | — |
| | | 1,633 | 34·74 | 117 | 3 | 39·00 |
| 1934 K. | .. | 2,447 | 53·19 | 171 | 3 | 57·00 |
| | | 2,643 | 48·05 | 212 | 6 | 35·33 |
| 1935 K. | .. | 2,339 | 41·76 | 32 | 1 | 32·00 |
| 1906-35 K. | .. | 39,658 | 42·55 | 28,252 | 1,526 | 18·51 |
| Gross Total | | 54,236 | 41·91 | 47,946 | 2,081 | 23·04 |

NOTE :—Played for Kent only in 1935.

## HUNDREDS HIT

IN this list are included only the centuries which I have scored in First-Class Cricket.

I am aware that there is some misunderstanding among statisticians that Two-Day matches shall not be reckoned as First-Class cricket.

In the absence of any official pronouncement on this matter from the only Authority qualified to make such pronouncement—viz., the Marylebone Cricket Club—I would point out that in the past many Two-Day Matches have been regarded as first-class matches. Also, that if Two-Day matches are not to be reckoned as First Class, then not only must we cancel out the whole of the season of 1919, but also the Test match at Manchester between England and Australia in 1921. That Test match was played under Two-Day Match Law, so cannot be held to have been a Three-Day Match unless Laws are meaningless.

Nor do I find it logical that two teams of First-Class Cricketers who play in a match from Monday to Wednesday make only Second-class runs if they engage in a match on Friday and Saturday.

Inasmuch as there is divergence of opinion in this matter, I hope that the only Authority on Cricket that matters will make its pronouncement, to which all Cricketers would immediately and gladly conform.

| 1906 | | |
|---|---|---|
| June 18–19 | Kent *v.* Hants (1) c Bacon b Badcock | 116 |

| 1908 | | |
|---|---|---|
| June 22–24 | Kent *v.* Northants (1) b Wells | 152 |
| Aug. 13–15 | Kent *v.* Somerset (1) b Robson | 105 |

**1909**

| | | |
|---|---|---|
| July 5–7 | Kent *v.* Worcester (1) c H. K. Foster b Arnold.. | 185 |
| July 22–24 | Kent *v.* Surrey (1) c Hayes b Rushby.......... | 117 |

**1910**

| | | |
|---|---|---|
| May 16–18 | Kent *v.* Middlesex (1) c Murrell b Mignon ...... | 120 |
| July 4–6 | Kent *v.* Sussex (1) b Leach .................. | 117 |
| Aug. 8–10 | Kent *v.* Somerset (2) c Robson b Hardy........ | 102 |

**1911**

| | | |
|---|---|---|
| July 10–11 | Kent *v.* Somerset (3) b Hardy ................ | 104 |
| July 10–11 | Kent *v.* Somerset (4) not out ............... | 148 |
| July 17–19 | Kent *v.* Worcester (2) c Bowley b Cuffe ........ | 119 |
| July 31– |  |  |
| Aug. 1 | Kent *v.* Sussex (2) not out..................... | 108 |
| Aug. 7–9 | Kent *v.* Hants (2) c and b McDonell .......... | 108 |
| Aug. 17–18 | Kent *v.* Gloucestershire (1) b Mills ............ | 148 |

**1912**

| | | |
|---|---|---|
| Jan. 26–29 | M.C.C. *v.* Tasmania not out .................. | 305 |
| Feb. 23–29, |  |  |
| Mar 1. | ENGLAND *v.* AUSTRALIA (1) not out ............ | 133 |
| May 23–25 | M.C.C. Australian XI *v.* the Rest b Dean ...... | 101 |
| June 27–29 | Kent *v.* Warwickshire (1) b Cliff .............. | 117 |

**1913**

| | | |
|---|---|---|
| May 19–21 | Kent *v.* Oxford University (1) not out ........ | 224 |
| June 26–28 | Kent *v.* Hants (3) c Jephson b Jaques ........ | 105 |
| July 3–5 | Kent *v.* Surrey (2) c Hobbs b Bird ............ | 177 |
| Aug 14–16 | Kent *v.* Somerset (5) not out.................. | 101 |
| Dec. 20–23 | M.C.C. *v.* Transvaal c Baumgartner b Dixon .... | 116 |

**1914**

| | | |
|---|---|---|
| May 28–30 | Kent *v.* Leicester (1) b Whitehead ............ | 147 |
| June 25–27 | Kent *v.* Leicester (2) c Coe b Shipman ........ | 117 |
| June 29–30, |  |  |
| July 1 | Kent *v.* Gloucestershire (2) not out ............ | 111 |
| July 20–22 | Kent *v.* Gloucestershire (3) b Dipper .......... | 120 |
| Aug. 17–19 | Kent *v.* Lancashire (1) c Dean b Sharp ........ | 101 |
| Aug. 20–22 | Kent *v.* Worcester (3) not out ................ | 160 |

**1919**

| | | |
|---|---|---|
| Aug. 11–12 | Kent *v.* Hants (4) c Jameson b Kennedy ...... | 134 |
| Aug. 15–16 | Kent *v.* Sussex (3) c Cox b R. Relf ............ | 107 |
| Sept. 15–18 | The Rest *v.* Yorkshire (1) run out ............ | 164 |

**1920**

| | | |
|---|---|---|
| May 24–26 | Kent v. Hants (5) c Mead b Kennedy .......... | 158 |
| June 26–29 | Kent v. Sussex (4) not out .................... | 139 |
| July 21–23 | Kent v. Northants (2) c Buswell b Wells ....... | 150 |
| Aug. 21–24 | Kent v. Essex (1) lbw b Russell ............... | 133 |
| Sept. 9–11 | M.C.C. Aust. XI v. Mr. C. I. Thornton's XI c Holmes b Hirst ..................... | 105 |

**1921**

| | | |
|---|---|---|
| Jan. 7–8 | M.C.C. v. Ballarat not out ..................... | 159 |
| Feb. 18–22 | M.C.C. v. N.S.W. b Hendry .................... | 138 |
| June 1–3 | Kent v. Warwickshire (2) lbw b Calthorpe ..... | 149 |
| June 8–10 | Kent v. Leicester (3) c Geary b Shipman ...... | 103 |
| June 15–16 | Kent v. Worcester (4) c Humpherson b Pearson . | 111 |
| July 20–21 | Kent v. Gloucestershire (4) b Mills ............. | 174 |
| Aug. 24–26 | Kent v. Middlesex (2) run out ................. | 103 |
| Aug. 27–30 | Kent v. Notts (1) b Staples ................... | 109 |

**1922**

| | | |
|---|---|---|
| May 17–19 | Kent v. Somerset (6) not out ................. | 102 |
| June 3–6 | Kent v. Hants (6) c & b Newman .............. | 188 |
| June 28–30 | Kent v. Leicester (4) st Sidwell b Astill........ | 123 |
| July 29–31, Aug. 1 | Kent v. Surrey (3) lbw b Shepherd ........... | 100 |
| Aug. 19–22 | Kent v. Lancashire (2) b Watson .............. | 155 |

**1923**

| | | |
|---|---|---|
| Feb. 9–13 | ENGLAND v. SOUTH AFRICA (1) not out ........ | 115 |
| May 12–15 | Kent v. Oxford Univ. (2) c Knott b Blaikie..... | 107 |
| June 20–22 | Kent v. Yorkshire (2) c Macaulay b Robinson ... | 138 |
| July 14–16 | Kent v. Leicester (5) not out .................. | 136 |
| Aug. 8–10 | Kent v. Middlesex (3) c Allen b Guise.......... | 270 |
| Aug. 11–14 | Kent v. Somerset (7) not out ................. | 106 |

**1924**

| | | |
|---|---|---|
| May 10–13 | Kent v. Essex (2) not out .................... | 117 |
| June 28–30, July 1 | ENGLAND v. SOUTH AFRICA (2) not out ....... | 134 |
| July 5–8 | Kent v. Sussex (5) c Watson b Wensley........ | 117 |
| July 23–25 | Kent v. Leicester (6) b Shipman................ | 141 |
| Aug. 2–5 | Kent v. Hants (7) b Brown ................... | 101 |
| Aug. 9–11 | Kent v. Sussex (6) c Parks b Tate ............. | 108 |
| Aug. 23–25 | Kent v. South Africa run out ................. | 176 |
| Sept. 13–16 | The Rest v. Yorkshire (3) st Dolphin b Macaulay | 202 |
| Dec. 19–27 | ENGLAND v. AUSTRALIA (2) c Mailey b Gregory .. | 123 |

**1925**

| | | |
|---|---|---|
| Feb. 21–25 | M.C.C. v. N.S.W. st Ratcliffe b Mailey ......... | 149 |
| May 9–11 | Kent v. Somerset (8) b Barlow ............... | 215 |
| June 20–22 | Kent v. Warwickshire (3) c Smith b Calthorpe .. | 136 |
| Aug. 5–7 | Kent v. Sussex (7) c Watson b Wensley ....... | 118 |
| Aug. 15–17 | Kent v. Gloucestershire (5) c Melsome b Mills .. | 176 |
| Sept. 12–16 | The Rest v. Yorkshire (4) c Oldroyd b Rhodes .. | 104 |

1926

| | | |
|---|---|---|
| June 23–25 | Kent *v.* Notts (2) c Lilley b Barratt .......... | 114 |
| June 30– | | |
| July 1–2 | Kent *v.* Lancashire (3) lbw b Watson .......... | 137 |
| July 21–23 | Kent *v.* Leicester (7) b Bale .................. | 106 |
| Aug. 7–10 | Kent *v.* Sussex (8) b Cox .................... | 104 |
| Aug. 28–31 | Kent *v.* Northants (3) lbw b Nicholson ........ | 217 |
| Sept. 11–14 | The Rest *v.* Lancashire (4) not out .......... | 172 |

1927

| | | |
|---|---|---|
| May 11–13 | Kent *v.* Derby (1) c Shardlow b Townsend...... | 187 |
| June 8–10 | Kent *v.* Northants (4) not out ................ | 106 |
| Aug. 27–30 | Kent *v.* Essex (3) c Wykes b Franklin ........ | 101 |

1927

| | | |
|---|---|---|
| Aug. 31– | | |
| Sept. 1–2 | Kent *v.* New Zealand (1) st James b Merritt .... | 125 |
| Sept. 7–9 | Kent *v.* M.C.C. (1) not out................... | 141 |

1928

| | | |
|---|---|---|
| May 9–11 | Kent *v.* Oxford Univ. (3) c Tew b Garland-Wells | 100 |
| May 23–25 | Kent *v.* Gloucestershire (6) b Sinfield .......... | 107 |
| June 9–12 | Kent *v.* Sussex (9) c Sellar b A. Gilligan........ | 128 |
| June 13–14 | Kent *v.* Warwickshire (4) b Howell ............ | 156 |
| June 20–22 | Kent *v.* Essex (4) not out ................... | 102 |
| July 4–6 | Kent *v.* Leicestershire (8) c Berry b Skelding.... | 160 |
| July 21–24 | Kent *v.* Derbyshire (2) c Townsend b Hutchinson | 198 |
| Aug. 11–14 | Kent *v.* Sussex (10) c Bowley b Browne ........ | 120 |
| Aug. 15–17 | Kent *v.* Lancashire (5) c Iddon b Macdonald.... | 151 |
| Sept. 1–4 | An England XI *v.* W. Indies (1) hit wkt b Francis ............................... | 151 |
| Sept. 5–7 | Kent *v.* M.C.C. (2) c Holmes b Newman ...... | 125 |
| Sept. 8–11 | Players *v.* Gentlemen (1) not out ............. | 141 |

1929

| | | |
|---|---|---|
| June 22–25 | Kent *v.* Derbyshire (3) c & b Smith............ | 155 |
| June 26–27 | Kent *v.* Somerset (9) b J. W. Lee............. | 108 |
| June 29, | | |
| July 1–2 | Kent *v.* Yorkshire (5) c Broadhurst b Rhodes .. | 131 |
| July 6–9 | Kent *v.* Hants (8) c Brown b Newman ........ | 117 |
| July 27–30 | England *v.* S. Africa (2) c & b Vincent ...... | 154 |
| Aug. 3–6 | Kent *v.* Gloucestershire (7) lbw b Sinfield ...... | 119 |
| Aug. 28–30 | Kent *v.* Middlesex (4) c Hearne b Lee.......... | 176 |
| Aug. 31, | | |
| Sept. 2–3 | Kent *v.* Essex (5) c Nichols b Raison .......... | 118 |
| Sept. 4–6 | Kent *v.* M.C.C. (3) c Brown b Durston ........ | 142 |
| Sept. 7–9 | An England XI *v.* S. Africa (3) b Bell........ | 111 |
| Sept. 13–18 | The Rest *v.* Notts (3) b Barratt .............. | 106 |
| Nov. 8–12 | M.C.C. *v.* S. Australia c Pritchard b Whitfield .. | 146 |
| Nov. 22–26 | M.C.C. *v.* N.S.W. b Fairfax .................. | 219 |

1930

Dec. 31,
Jan. 1–2    M.C.C. *v.* Otago c Clark b Elmes ............. 132
Jan. 16–18  M.C.C. *v.* Manawata b Cutler ................ 125
May 24–27   Kent *v.* Yorkshire (6) c Barber b Bowes........ 119
July 5–8    Kent *v.* Sussex (11) c Hammond b Langridge (Jas.) 120
July 12–15  Kent *v.* Surrey (4) c Allom b Peach............ 110
July 26–29  Kent *v.* Surrey (5) c Brooks b Gover .......... 109

1931

May 27–29   Kent *v.* Lancashire (6) c Tyldesley (R.) b Macdonald 108
May 30,
June 1–2    Kent *v.* Yorkshire (7) c Sutcliffe b Leyland  .... 188
June 10–12  Kent *v.* Northants (5) c Bellamy b Matthews  .. 168
June 24–25  Kent *v.* Warwickshire (5) not out  ............ 103
Aug. 16–19  Kent *v.* Lancashire (7) c Sibbles b Hopwood  .. 103
Aug. 26–28  Kent *v.* New Zealand (2) c Blunt b Vivian...... 224

1932

June 4–7    Kent *v.* Glamorgan (1) c Turnball b Clay  ...... 146

1933

June 28–30  Kent *v.* Somerset (10) b J. W. Lee ............ 198
july 19–21  Kent *v.* Middlesex (5) run out ................ 108
July 25–28  Kent *v.* Leicestershire (9) c Astill b Shipman.... 131
Aug. 9–11   Kent *v.* Derbyshire (4) c Elliott b Worthington  161
Sept. 2–5   AN ENGLAND XI *v.* W. INDIES b. Grant........ 136

1934

May 19–22   Kent *v.* Somerset (11) st Luckes b Buse ........ 121
May 30–
June 1      Kent *v.* Essex (6) b C. T. Ashton  ............ 172
June 2–5    Kent *v.* Yorkshire (8) st Wood b Hutton  ...... 106
June 13–15  Kent *v.* Worcestershire (5) c Gibbons b Brook  .. 104
June 30–
July 2      Kent *v.* Gloucestershire (8) st Hopkins b Sinfield 124
July 7–10   Kent *v.* Hants (9) c Drake b Creese............ 122
July 14–17  Kent *v.* Surrey (6) lbw b Watts  .............. 132
July 18–20  Kent *v.* Northants (6) c Clark b Cox  .......... 176
Aug. 8–10   Kent *v.* Notts (4) c Gunn b Butler ............ 101
Aug. 15–17  Kent *v.* Northants (7) c Cox b Knight  ........ 104

1935

May 1–3     Kent *v.* Leicestershire (10) c Prentice b Smith, H.D. 105
June 8–11   Kent *v.* Gloucestershire (9) c Hammond b Goddard 110
July 3–5    Kent *v.* Sussex (12) c Melville b J. Cornford .... 172
July 27–30  Kent *v.* Surrey (7) b Brown .................. 229
Aug. 10–13  Kent *v.* Sussex (13) c Langridge (John) b Parks (J.) 157
Sept. 7–10  Kent *v.* M.C.C. (4) lbw b Read ................ 117

## TEST MATCH CENTURIES

1912  Feb. 23–29,
         Mar. 1—ENGLAND *v.* AUSTRALIA, not out ............ 133
1923  Feb.  9–13—ENGLAND *v.* S. AFRICA, not out ............. 115
1924  June 28–30,
         July 1—ENGLAND *v.* S. AFRICA, not out ............... 134
1924  Dec. 19–27—ENGLAND *v.* AUSTRALIA, c Mailey b Gregory 123
1929  July 27–30—ENGLAND *v.* S. AFRICA, c & b Vincent ...... 154

## AN ENGLAND XI CENTURIES

1928  Sept. 1–4—*v.* W. Indies, hit wkt. b. Francis.............. 151
1929  Sept. 7–9—*v.* S. Africa, b Bell ................................. 111
1933  Sept. 2–5—*v.* W. Indies, b Grant ............................ 136

## FOR REST OF ENGLAND *v.* CHAMPION COUNTY

1919  Sept. 15–18—*v.* Yorkshire, run out ......................... 164
1924  Sept. 13–16—*v.* Yorkshire, st Dolphin b Macauley ....... 202
1925  Sept. 12–16—*v.* Yorkshire, c Oldroyd b Rhodes .......... 104
1926  Sept. 11–14—*v.* Lancashire, not out ........................ 172
1929  Sept. 14–18—*v.* Notts, b Barratt ............................. 106

## FOR PLAYERS

1928  Sept. 8–11—*v.* Gentlemen, not out ......................... 141

## CENTURIES OVER 200

1912  Jan. 26–29—M.C.C. *v.* Tasmania, not out ................. 305
1913  May 19–21—Kent *v.* Oxford Univ., not out .............. 224
1923  Aug.  8–10—Kent *v.* Middlesex, c Allen b Guise.......... 270
1924  Sept. 13–16—Rest *v.* Yorkshire, st Dolphin b Macaulay 202
1925  May  9–11—Kent *v.* Somerset, b Barlow ................. 215
1926  Aug. 28–31—Kent *v.* Northants, lbw b Nicholson......... 217
1929  Nov. 22–26—M.C.C. *v.* N.S.W., b Fairfax ................. 219
1931  Aug. 26–28—Kent *v.* New Zealand, c Blunt b Vivian ... 224
1935  July 27–30—Kent *v.* Surrey, b Brown ...................... 229

## CENTURIES AGAINST ODD TEAMS

1912  Jan. 26–29—M.C.C. *v.* Tasmania, not out ................. 305
1912  May 23–25—M.C.C. Australian XI *v.* The Rest, b Dean 101
1920  Sept. 9–11—M.C.C. Australian XI *v.* Mr. C. I. Thorn-
                          ton's XI, c Holmes b Hirst ... 105

## CENTURIES AGAINST THE UNIVERSITIES

1913  May 19–21—Kent *v.* Oxford, not out ........................ 224
1923  May 12–15—Kent *v.* Oxford, c Knott b Blaikie .......... 107
1928  May  9–11—Kent *v.* Oxford, c Tew b Garland Wells ... 100

## CENTURIES ON DIFFERENT GROUNDS

| | | | | | |
|---|---:|---|---|---|---:|
| Adelaide ... ... ... | 1 | Horsham ... ... ... | 1 |
| Ashby de la Zouch ... ... | 1 | Johannesburg ... ... | 2 |
| Ballarat ... ... ... | 1 | Kennington Oval ... ... | 8 |
| Birmingham ... ... | 2 | Leeds ... ... ... | 2 |
| Blackheath ... ... ... | 4 | Leyton ... ... ... | 4 |
| Bournemouth ... ... | 1 | Leicester ... ... | 2 |
| Bradford ... ... ... | 1 | Lord's ... ... ... | 5 |
| Brentwood ... ... ... | 1 | Maidstone ... ... | 8 |
| Bristol ... ... ... | 1 | Manchester ... ... | 3 |
| Brighton ... ... ... | 2 | Nottingham ... ... | 2 |
| Canterbury ... ... ... | 11 | Northampton ... ... | 3 |
| Catford ... ... ... | 1 | Oxford ... ... ... | 3 |
| Chatham ... ... ... | 1 | Portsmouth ... ... | 1 |
| Cheltenham ... ... | 2 | Palmerston North ... | 1 |
| Chesterfield ... ... | 1 | Scarborough... ... | 1 |
| Dover ... ... ... | 5 | Southampton ... ... | 2 |
| Dudley ... ... ... | 1 | Stourbridge ... ... | 1 |
| Dunedin ... ... ... | 1 | Swansea ... ... | 1 |
| Folkestone ... ... | 12 | Sydney ... ... ... | 5 |
| Gloucester ... ... | 2 | Taunton ... ... | 4 |
| Gravesend ... ... | 5 | Tonbridge ... ... | 9 |
| Hastings ... ... | 5 | Tunbridge Wells ... | 8 |
| Hobart ... ... ... | 1 | Weston-super-Mare... ... | 1 |

## BEST BOWLING PERFORMANCES

| | | Inns | O | M | R | W |
|---|---|---|---|---|---|---|
| **1906** | | | | | | |
| June 14–15—Oval, Kent v. Surrey | | 2 | 24·3 | 7 | 39 | 6 |
| June 18–19—Tonbridge, Kent v. Hants | | 2 | 21 | 8 | 46 | 6 |
| **1908** | | | | | | |
| Aug. 24–26—Lord's, Kent v. Middlesex | | 2 | 4·3 | 2 | 8 | 6 |
| Aug. 27–29—Canterbury, | | | | | | |
| | Kent v. Philadelphians... | 1 | 29·5 | 9 | 75 | 7 |
| **1909** | | | | | | |
| July 29–31—Leyton, Kent v. Essex | | 1 | 19·4 | 4 | 42 | 7 |
| **1910** | | | | | | |
| July 4–6 —Hastings, Kent v. Sussex | | 2 | 27·4 | 11 | 52 | 8 |
| **1911** | | | | | | |
| June 15–17—Tonbridge, Kent v. Northants | | 2 | 27·5 | 6 | 61 | 7 |
| June 26–28—Dover, Kent v. Notts | | 2 | 15 | 2 | 42 | 6 |
| Aug. 21–23—Oval, Kent v. Surrey | | 2 | 6·3 | 3 | 9 | 7 |
| **1912** | | | | | | |
| May 20–22—Leeds, Kent v. Yorkshire | | 1 | 20·4 | 7 | 42 | 6 |
| June 3– 5—Nottingham, Kent v. Notts | | 1 | 18·2 | 9 | 21 | 6 |
| July 1– 3—Gravesend, Kent v. Essex | | 2 | 17 | 8 | 25 | 7 |
| Aug. 1– 3—Leyton, Kent v. Essex | | 2 | 24 | 5 | 70 | 6 |
| Aug. 19–22—Oval, ENGLAND v. AUSTRALIA | | 2 | 17·2 | 4 | 49 | 10 |
| **1913** | | | | | | |
| June 9–10—Stourbridge, Kent v. Worcester | | 1 | 10 | 2 | 31 | 6 |
| July 21–22—Maidstone, Kent v. Lancashire | | 2 | 17 | 5 | 33 | 6 |
| Dec. 8–10—Pietermaritzburg, M.C.C. v. | | | | | | |
| | Natal | 1 | 15 | 1 | 41 | 6 |
| **1924** | | | | | | |
| May 9–11—Lord's, Kent v. M.C.C. | | 2 | 21 | 4 | 56 | 7 |
| June 29–30, | | | | | | |
| July 1—Gloucester, Kent v. Gloucester | | 1 | 21·2 | 7 | 66 | 7 |
| July 23–24—Maidstone, Kent v. Middlesex | | 2 | 21 | 7 | 54 | 7 |
| **1919** | | | | | | |
| June 9–10—Leyton, Kent v. Essex | | 1 | 30·5 | 8 | 74 | 6 |
| June 20–21—Tonbridge, Kent v. Sussex | | 1 | 13 | 3 | 33 | 6 |
| June 20–21—Tonbridge, Kent v. Sussex | | 2 | 20·1 | 8 | 28 | 6 |
| June 27–28—Manchester, Kent v. Lancs. | | 1 | 12·3 | 1 | 44 | 6 |
| July 3– 5—Oval, Players v. Gentlemen | | 1 | 30 | 4 | 69 | 6 |
| July 25–26—Blackheath, Kent v. Surrey | | 1 | 71·1 | 6 | 36 | 7 |
| July 30–31—Maidstone, Kent v. Middlesex | | 1 | 25 | 10 | 54 | 6 |
| Sept. 1– 3—Hastings, The South v. | | | | | | |
| | Imperial Forces | 1 | 31·3 | 10 | 74 | 6 |

1920
May   29–31,

| | | | | | |
|---|---|---|---|---|---|
| June  1—Leicester, Kent v. Leicester ... | 1 | 28·1 | 7 | 59 | 7 |
| June 10–14—Tonbridge, Kent v. Worcester | 1 | 14 | 4 | 30 | 6 |
| June 19–21—Gravesend, Kent v. Gloucester | 2 | 11 | 4 | 31 | 6 |
| June 26–29—Horsham, Kent v. Sussex ...... | 1 | 34 | 10 | 52 | 6 |
| July 21–23—Maidstone, Kent v. Northants | 1 | 16·1 | 4 | 41 | 6 |
| July 28–30—Northampton, Kent v. Northants | 2 | 21·3 | 5 | 56 | 6 |
| July 31, |||||
| Aug.  2—Canterbury, Kent v. Hants ... | 1 | 26 | 13 | 35 | 6 |
| Aug.  7–10—Clifton, Kent v. Gloucester ... | 2 | 35 | 8 | 76 | 7 |

1921

| | | | | | |
|---|---|---|---|---|---|
| July 20–21—Maidstone, Kent v. Gloucester | 1 | 11·5 | 4 | 22 | 8 |
| July 30, |||||
| Aug.  1–2—Canterbury, Kent v. Hants ... | 1 | 14 | 4 | 28 | 6 |
| Aug. 20–23—Dover, Kent v. Northants ...... | 2 | 14·2 | 3 | 20 | 7 |
| Aug. 27–30—Nottingham, Kent v. Notts ... | 1 | 28·4 | 13 | 40 | 7 |
| Sept. 12–15—Oval, The Rest v. Middlesex ... | 2 | 30·4 | 7 | 68 | 8 |

1922

| | | | | | |
|---|---|---|---|---|---|
| June  3–6 —Southampton, Kent v. Hants | 1 | 30·2 | 5 | 97 | 6 |
| June 17–19—Kidderminster, Kent v. Worcs | 2 | 15 | 6 | 31 | 6 |
| July  1– 4—Birmingham, Kent v. Warwick | 1 | 18 | 4 | 52 | 8 |
| July  1– 4—Birmingham, Kent v. Warwick | 2 | 13 | 4 | 39 | 6 |
| July  8–10—Tunbridge Wells, |||||
| Kent v. Northants ... | 1 | 27·2 | 4 | 87 | 6 |
| July 15–17—Maidstone, Kent v. Warwick... | 1 | 18 | 5 | 38 | 6 |
| Aug.  9–11—Canterbury, Kent v. Middlesex | 1 | 27 | 12 | 34 | 7 |
| Aug.  9–11—Canterbury, Kent v. Middlesex | 2 | 28 | 12 | 45 | 6 |
| Aug. 12–15—Taunton, Kent v. Somerset ... | 1 | 21 | 7 | 53 | 6 |
| Nov. 25–27—East London, |||||
| M.C.C. v. The Border | 2 | 19·5 | 6 | 43 | 6 |

1923

| | | | | | |
|---|---|---|---|---|---|
| June  6– 8—Leyton, Kent v. Essex ......... | 1 | 37 | 13 | 84 | 6 |
| June  6– 8—Leyton, Kent v. Essex ......... | 2 | 17 | 10 | 21 | 6 |
| Aug. 29–31—Lord's, Kent v. Middlesex ...... | 1 | 44·1 | 15 | 91 | 6 |

1924

| | | | | | |
|---|---|---|---|---|---|
| May 21–23—Oxford, Kent v. Oxford Univ. | 1 | 21 | 7 | 40 | 6 |
| July  9–10—Tunbridge Wells, |||||
| Kent v. Leicester...... | 1 | 16·5 | 7 | 29 | 6 |

1928

| | | | | | |
|---|---|---|---|---|---|
| June 13–14—Tunbridge Wells, |||||
| Kent v. Warwick......... | 2 | 15·2 | 5 | 52 | 6 |

1930
Dec 31,

| | | | | | |
|---|---|---|---|---|---|
| Jan. 1– 2—Dunedin, M.C.C. v. Otago ...... | 1 | 28 | 9 | 50 | 6 |
| Jan.  4– 6—Invercargill—M.C.C. v. Southend | 1 | 23 | 5 | 50 | 6 |
| Jan. 24–27—Wellington, |||||
| ENGLAND v. NEW ZEALAND | 1 | 28·3 | 5 | 76 | 7 |

## HOW OUT

| | To end of 1933 | | In 1934 | | In 1935 | | Total |
|---|---|---|---|---|---|---|---|
| Bowled ... | ... | 350 | ... | 11 | ... | 15 | ... | 376 |
| Caught ... | ... | 618 | ... | 35 | ... | 30 | ... | 683 |
| L.B.W. ... | ... | 139 | ... | 6 | ... | 9 | ... | 154 |
| L.B.W. (N.) | ... | — | ... | — | ... | 1 | ... | 1 |
| Not Out ... | ... | 80 | ... | 1 | ... | 0 | ... | 81 |
| Run Out ... | ... | 38 | ... | 0 | ... | 1 | ... | 39 |
| Stumped ... | ... | 36 | ... | 3 | ... | 0 | ... | 39 |
| Hit Wicket | ... | 7 | ... | 0 | ... | 0 | ... | 7 |
| Retired ... | ... | 1 | ... | 0 | ... | 0 | ... | 1 |
| Retired Hurt | ... | 3 | ... | 0 | ... | 0 | ... | 3 |
| Duck's Eggs | ... | 82 | ... | 2 | ... | 2 | ... | 86 |

## CATCHES MADE

| 908 | ... | 42 | ... | 44 | ... | 994 |
|---|---|---|---|---|---|---|

## MY 64 TESTS

|  |  |  |  | O | M | R | W |
|---|---|---|---|---|---|---|---|
| **1909** | | | | | | | |
| Aug. 9–11—AUSTRALIA, 5th Test, b Cotter . | | | 8 | 4 | 1 | 6 | 0 |
| | Oval. | | | 6 | 0 | 31 | 0 |
| | | | | | | | |
| **1910** | | | | | | | |
| Jan. 1– 5—S. AFRICA, 1st Test | | | | | | | |
| | c Schway b Vogler | ...... | 14 | 1 | 0 | 4 | 0 |
| | Johannesburg. b Vogler | .... | 25 | 4 | 1 | 13 | 0 |
| Jan. 21–26—S. AFRICA, 2nd Test | | | | | | | |
| | c Zulch b Vogler | ......... | 22 | 15 | 5 | 23 | 1 |
| | Durban c Vogler b Faulkner . | | 4 | 10 | 3 | 34 | 1 |
| Feb. 26–28, | | | | | | | |
| Mar. 1—S. AFRICA, 3rd Test | | | | | | | |
| | not out | .................. | 58 | 21 | 4 | 54 | 1 |
| | Johannesburg c Nourse b Vogler | | 0 | 18 | 6 | 29 | 0 |
| Mar. 7–9 —S. AFRICA, 4th Test | | | | | | | |
| | c Zulch b Sinclair | .... | 69 | 6 | 2 | 23 | 1 |
| | Cape Town. b Vogler | ......... | 64 | 3 | 0 | 24 | 0 |
| Mar. 11–15—S. AFRICA, 5th Test | | | | | | | |
| | b Norton | ............ | 0 | – | – | – | – |
| | Cape Town | | | 13 | 3 | 47 | 3 |
| | | | | | | | |
| **1911** | | | | | | | |
| Dec. 15–21—AUSTRALIA, 1st Test | | | | | | | |
| | b Hordern | ....,... | 39 | 21 | 1 | 77 | 2 |
| | Sydney. c Armstrong b Cotter | | 7 | 6 | 1 | 15 | 0 |
| | | | | | | | |
| **1912** | | | | | | | |
| Dec. 30, | | | | | | | |
| Jan. 1–3—AUSTRALIA, 2nd Test | | | | | | | |
| | c Ransford b Hordern | .... | 23 | 0·1 | 0 | 0 | 1 |
| | Melbourne. | | | 3 | 0 | 21 | 0 |
| Jan. 12–17—AUSTRALIA, 3rd Test | | | | | | | |
| | b Cotter | ..................... | 20 | – | – | – | – |
| | Adelaide. | | | 7 | 1 | 30 | 0 |
| Feb. 9–13—AUSTRALIA, 4th Test | | | | | | | |
| | c Kelleway b Minnett | .... | 56 | 11 | 3 | 22 | 1 |
| | Melbourne. | | | 2 | 0 | 7 | 0 |
| Feb. 23–29, | | | | | | | |
| Mar. 1—AUSTRALIA, 5th Test | | | | | | | |
| | not out | ................. | 133 | 2 | 1 | 1 | 2 |
| | Sydney. c Armstrong b Hazlitt | | 11 | 16 | 5 | 36 | 1 |
| June 10–12—S. AFRICA, 1st Test | | | | | | | |
| | b Pegler | ............... | 73 | – | – | – | – |
| | Lord's. | | — | 4 | 0 | 19 | 0 |
| June 24–26—AUSTRALIA, 1st Test | | | | | | | |
| | c Kelleway b Hazlitt | ...... | 20 | – | – | – | – |
| | Lord's. | | — | – | – | – | – |

**1912**

| | O | M | R | W |
|---|---|---|---|---|
| July   8–10—S. AFRICA, 2nd Test | | | | |
| b Nourse .............. 57 | 6 | 2 | 13 | 1 |
| Leeds.   c Nourse b Pegler ...   4 | – | – | – | – |
| July  29–31—AUSTRALIA, 2nd Test | | | | |
| c Kelleway b Whitty ... 13 | 6 | 3 | 6 | 0 |
| Manchester.　　　　　　— | – | – | – | – |
| Aug.  12–13—S. AFRICA, 3rd Test | | | | |
| b Pegler ................. 13 | 15·3 | 1 | 41 | 5 |
| Oval.　　　　　　　— | 9 | 2 | 24 | 1 |
| Aug.  19–22—AUSTRALIA, 3rd Test | | | | |
| lbw b Minnett ............ 62 | 9·4 | 3 | 29 | 5 |
| Oval.　　　　b Hazlitt ............ 4 | 7·4 | 1 | 20 | 5 |

**1913**

| | O | M | R | W |
|---|---|---|---|---|
| Dec.  13–17—S. AFRICA, 1st Test | | | | |
| c Cooper b Hartigan ... 31 | 7 | 0 | 24 | 1 |
| Durban.　　　　　— | 9 | 3 | 16 | 2 |
| Dec.  26–30—S. AFRICA, 2nd Test | | | | |
| b Newbury .............. 0 | 3 | 1 | 5 | 1 |
| Johannesburg.　　— | 21 | 5 | 45 | 0 |
| **1914** | | | | |
| Jan.  1– 5—S. AFRICA, 3rd Test | | | | |
| lbw b Taylor ............ 7 | 5 | 1 | 13 | 0 |
| Johannesburg. | | | | |
| st Ward b Newbury ... 37 | 7 | 0 | 24 | 0 |
| Feb.  14–18—S. AFRICA, 4th Test | | | | |
| c Hands b Newbury ... 9 | 10 | 3 | 27 | 0 |
| Durban.　　not out ......... 0 | 13 | 2 | 26 | 0 |
| Feb.  27–28, | | | | |
| Mar.  2–3—S. AFRICA, 5th Test | | | | |
| lbw b Newbury ......... 54 | 22 | 4 | 71 | 3 |
| Port Elizabeth.　　— | 5 | 2 | 23 | 0 |

**1920**

| | O | M | R | W |
|---|---|---|---|---|
| Dec.  17–22—AUSTRALIA, 1st Test | | | | |
| c Mailey b Ryder ...... 52 | 23 | 7 | 35 | 2 |
| Sydney.   st Oldfield b Mailey 16 | 23 | 11 | 90 | 2 |
| Dec.  31, | | | | |
| Jan.  1–4—AUSTRALIA, 2nd Test | | | | |
| b Gregory... 5 | 27 | 8 | 87 | 2 |
| Melbourne.　　b Ryder ... 50 | – | – | – | – |
| Jan.  14–20—AUSTRALIA, 3rd Test | | | | |
| c Kelleway b Gregory... 79 | 21 | 6 | 47 | 0 |
| Adelaide.　　　b Gregory...... 0 | 38 | 4 | 91 | 0 |
| Feb.  11–16—AUSTRALIA, 4th Test | | | | |
| lbw b Kelleway ......... 29 | 32·1 | 14 | 56 | 3 |
| Melbourne.  st Carter b Mailey 0 | 14 | 4 | 39 | 0 |
| Feb.  25–28, | | | | |
| Mar.  1—AUSTRALIA, 5th Test | | | | |
| b Macdonald ............ 53 | 15 | 1 | 58 | 0 |
| Sydney.   c & b Kelleway ...... 1 | 11 | 3 | 27 | 0 |

**1920**

May  28–30—AUSTRALIA, 1st Test

|  |  | O | M | R | W |
|---|---|---|---|---|---|
| c Hendry b Macdonald | 20 | 22 | 8 | 46 | 3 |
| Nottingham. c Carter b Hendry | 34 | – | – | – | – |

June 11–14—AUSTRALIA, 2nd Test

|  |  | O | M | R | W |
|---|---|---|---|---|---|
| st Carter b Mailey ...... | 95 | 11 | 2 | 44 | 0 |
| Lord's.  c Hendry b Mailey ... | 93 | 3 | 0 | 10 | 0 |

July  2– 5—AUSTRALIA, 3rd Test

|  |  | O | M | R | W |
|---|---|---|---|---|---|
| b Gregory ...... | 0 | 5 | 0 | 34 | 1 |
| Leeds.        b Mailey ......... | 37 | 18 | 4 | 43 | 1 |

July 23–26—AUSTRALIA, 4th Test

|  |  | O | M | R | W |
|---|---|---|---|---|---|
| c Pellew b Armstrong... | 41 | 39 | 22 | 38 | 0 |
| Manchester. | — | – | – | – | – |

Aug. 13–16—AUSTRALIA, 5th Test

|  |  | O | M | R | W |
|---|---|---|---|---|---|
| Oval.         run out ......| 23 | 11 | 2 | 31 | 2 |

**1922**

Dec. 23–28—S. AFRICA, 1st Test

|  |  | O | M | R | W |
|---|---|---|---|---|---|
| lbw b Francois............ | 26 | – | – | – | – |
| c Nupen b Francois  ... | 15 | 15 | 4 | 33 | 0 |
| Johannesburg. |  |  |  |  |  |

**1923**

Jan.  1– 4—S. AFRICA, 2nd Test

|  |  | O | M | R | W |
|---|---|---|---|---|---|
| c Francois b Hall  ...... | 0 | 2 | 1 | 1 | 0 |
| Cape Town.  b Hall ............ | 5 | 11 | 3 | 22 | 0 |

Jan. 18–22—S. AFRICA, 3rd Test

|  |  | O | M | R | W |
|---|---|---|---|---|---|
| c Nourse b Hall ......... | 0 | 15 | 3 | 47 | 0 |
| Durban. | — | – | – | – | – |

Feb.  9–13—S. AFRICA, 4th Test

|  |  | O | M | R | W |
|---|---|---|---|---|---|
| c Nourse b Hall ......... | 15 | 6 | 3 | 10 | 0 |
| Johannesburg.  not out ...... | 15 | 6 | 2 | 26 | 0 |

Feb. 16–22—S. AFRICA, 5th Test

|  |  | O | M | R | W |
|---|---|---|---|---|---|
| c & b Meintjes ........ | 2 | 6 | 3 | 9 | 0 |
| Durban.  c Nourse b Snooke | 8 | 3 | 2 | 3 | 0 |

**1924**

June 14–17—S. AFRICA, 1st Test

|  |  | O | M | R | W |
|---|---|---|---|---|---|
| c Ward b Parker  ...... | 64 | – | – | – | – |
| Birmingham. | — | 10 | 2 | 41 | 0 |

June 28–30,
July  1—S. AFRICA, 2nd Test

|  |  | O | M | R | W |
|---|---|---|---|---|---|
| not out ..................... | 134 | – | – | – | – |
| Lord's. | — | 4 | 1 | 9 | 0 |

July 12–15—S. AFRICA, 3rd Test

|  |  | O | M | R | W |
|---|---|---|---|---|---|
| b Pegler  ................. | 0 | – | – | – | – |
| Leeds. | — | 9 | 2 | 21 | 0 |

July 26–29—S. AFRICA, 4th Test, did not bat

|  |  | O | M | R | W |
|---|---|---|---|---|---|
| Manchester. | — | – | – | – | – |

Aug. 16–19—S. AFRICA, 5th Test

|  |  | O | M | R | W |
|---|---|---|---|---|---|
| b Carter  ................... | 51 | 14 | 4 | 22 | 1 |
| Oval. | — | – | – | – | – |

1924

| Dec. 19-27—AUSTRALIA, 1st Test | | O | M | R | W |
|---|---|---|---|---|---|
| b Gregory .................. | 0 | 9 | 0 | 35 | 0 |
| Sydney.   c Mailey b Gregory ...123 | | – | – | – | – |

1925

| Jan. 1- 8—AUSTRALIA, 2nd Test | | | | | |
|---|---|---|---|---|---|
| Melbourne.      b Gregory ....... | 0 | – | – | – | – |
| lbw b A. Richardson .. | 50 | 11 | 3 | 26 | 0 |

| Jan. 16-23—AUSTRALIA, 3rd Test | | | | | |
|---|---|---|---|---|---|
| c Andrews b Mailey ....... | 16 | 43 | 3 | 135 | 1 |
| Adelaide.       b Kelleway ...... | 21 | 19 | 1 | 77 | 4 |

| Feb. 13-18—AUSTRALIA, 4th Test | | | | | |
|---|---|---|---|---|---|
| st Oldfield b Mailey ...... | 40 | 9 | 1 | 53 | 1 |
| Melbourne. | | 6 | 0 | 17 | 1 |

Feb. 27-28,

| Mar. 2-4—AUSTRALIA, 5th Test | | | | | |
|---|---|---|---|---|---|
| b Grimmett .......... | 47 | 51 | 0 | 18 | 0 |
| Sydney.   c Andrews b Kelleway | 28 | 8 | 1 | 14 | 1 |

1926

| June 12-15—AUSTRALIA, 1st Test, did not bat | | – | – | – | – |
|---|---|---|---|---|---|
| Nottingham.   Rain drowned Test | | – | – | – | – |

| June 26-29—AUSTRALIA, 2nd Test | | | | | |
|---|---|---|---|---|---|
| lbw b Ryder ................ | 87 | 2 | 0 | 5 | 0 |
| Lord's. | | – | – | – | – |

| July 10-13—AUSTRALIA, 3rd Test | | | | | |
|---|---|---|---|---|---|
| run out .......... | 27 | – | – | – | – |
| Leeds.  c Macartney b Grimmett | 20 | – | – | – | – |

| July 24-27—AUSTRALIA, 4th Test | | | | | |
|---|---|---|---|---|---|
| c Ryder b Mailey ......... | 58 | 2 | 0 | 19 | 0 |
| Manchester.   No play first day | | – | – | – | – |

| Aug. 14-18—AUSTRALIA, 5th Test | | | | | |
|---|---|---|---|---|---|
| b Mailey .......... | 18 | – | – | – | – |
| Oval.      lbw b Richardson .... | 27 | – | – | – | – |

1929

| July 13-16—S. AFRICA, 3rd Test | | | | | |
|---|---|---|---|---|---|
| b Vincent .................... | 83 | – | – | – | – |
| Leeds.    not out ................. | 95 | 13·1 | 3 | 35 | 3 |

| July 27-30—S. AFRICA, 4th Test | | | | | |
|---|---|---|---|---|---|
| c & b Vincent............ | 154 | 9 | 3 | 22 | 0 |
| Manchester. | – | 18 | 5 | 51 | 1 |

| Aug. 17-20—S. AFRICA, 5th Test | | | | | |
|---|---|---|---|---|---|
| hit wkt. b Vincent ...... | 46 | 13 | 4 | 25 | 1 |
| Oval. | | – | – | – | – |

1930

| Jan. 10-13—NEW ZEALAND, 1st Test | | | | | |
|---|---|---|---|---|---|
| c Merritt b Dickinson .... | 31 | – | – | – | – |
| Christchurch.    not out ......... | 17 | 9 | 2 | 37 | 2 |

|            |                                          |    | O    | M  | R   | W |
|------------|------------------------------------------|----|------|----|-----|---|
| **1930**   |                                          |    |      |    |     |   |
| Jan. 24–27 | —NEW ZEALAND, 2nd Test                   |    |      |    |     |   |
|            | c Lowry b Dickinson ...                  | 6  | 28·3 | 5  | 76  | 7 |
|            | Wellington.           b Merritt ...      | 23 | 23   | 9  | 48  | 2 |
| Feb. 14–17 | —NEW ZEALAND, 3rd Test                   |    |      |    |     |   |
|            | run out .....................            | 59 | –    | –  | –   | – |
|            | Auckland.                                |    | –    | –  | –   | – |
| June 13–17 | —NEW ZEALAND, 4th Test                   |    |      |    |     |   |
|            | b Allcott ..................             | 10 | 41   | 10 | 100 | 2 |
|            | Nottingham.                              |    | –    | –  | –   | – |
| June 13–17 | —Australia, 1st Test                     |    |      |    |     |   |
|            | st Oldfield b Grimmett                   | 0  | –    | –  | –   | – |
|            | Nottingham.           b Wall.........    | 5  | 3    | 1  | 3   | 0 |
| June 27–30, July 1 | —AUSTRALIA, 2nd Test             |    |      |    |     |   |
|            | c Wall b Fairfax .........               | 41 | 6    | 0  | 35  | 0 |
|            | Lord's.   hit wkt. b Grimmett            | 28 | –    | –  | –   | – |
| **1931**   |                                          |    |      |    |     |   |
| June 27–30 | —NEW ZEALAND, 1st Test                   |    |      |    |     |   |
|            | lbw b Merritt .............              | 80 | –    | –  | –   | – |
|            | Lord's.           b Cromb .........      | 9  | –    | –  | –   | – |
| **1932**   |                                          |    |      |    |     |   |
| June 25–28 | —INDIA (only Test)                       |    |      |    |     |   |
|            | run out .............                    | 9  | –    | –  | –   | – |
|            | Lords.  c Colah b Jehangir Khan          | 21 | –    | –  | –   | – |
| **1934**   |                                          |    |      |    |     |   |
| Aug. 18–22 | —AUSTRALIA, 5th TEST                     |    |      |    |     |   |
|            | c McCabe b O'Reilly ...                  | 4  | –    | –  | –   | – |
|            | Oval.  c Ponsford b McCabe               | 0  | –    | –  | –   | – |